THE
EXTRA Edge

A Woman's Guide to
TOTAL Professional Style

THE
Success Strategies For Women
EXTRA Edge

Charlene Mitchell

with Thomas Burdick
Former Editor-in-Chief of The
HARVARD BUSINESS SCHOOL NEWSPAPER

Illustrations by Virginia Casey

ACROPOLIS BOOKS LTD.
Washington, D.C.
98517

ACROPOLIS BOOKS, LTD.
Colortone Building, 2400 17th St., N.W., Washington, D.C. 20009

Printed in the United States of America by
COLORTONE PRESS
Creative Graphics, Inc.
Washington, D.C. 20009

Attention: Schools and Corporations
ACROPOLIS books are available at quantity discounts with bulk purchase for educational, business, or sales promo-tional use. For information, please write to: SPECIAL SALES DEPARTMENT, ACROPOLIS BOOKS LTD., 2400 17th ST., N.W., WASHINGTON, D.C. 20009.

Are there Acropolis Books you want but cannot find in your local stores?
You can get any Acropolis book title in print. Simply send title and retail price, plus 50 cents per copy to cover mailing and handling costs for each book desired. District of Colum-bia residents add applicable sales tax. Enclose check or money order only, no cash please, to: ACROPOLIS BOOKS LTD., 2400 17th ST., N.W., WASHINGTON, D.C. 20009.

Library of Congress Cataloging in Publication Data

Mitchell, Charlene, 1950-
The extra edge.

1. Women executives. 2. Success. I. Burdick, Thomas, 1950-   . II. Title.
HF5500.2.M516 1983   658.4'09'024042   83-7138
ISBN 0-87491-606-2

Cover photo by H. Halliwell, Boston.

Acknowledgments

The authors would like to thank the following individuals for their assistance in this project:

John Noble and Kathy Fox at Harvard University, Sandy Berke and Dr. Robert Kent at the Harvard Business School, Dr. Roderick Hodgins, Nancy Muller and Diane Shaib at American Express, Dan Scheer at I.B.M., the Rhode Island School of Design, the staff at Catalyst in New York, Toby Field of Toby Field Associates of Newport, Harriet Davis of Merrill Lynch, Lufthansa German Airlines, Pat Patricelli and Susie Chin of Filene's of Boston.

We would also like to especially thank the staff at Acropolis Books for their support and encouragement. With special thanks to Kathleen Hughes, our editor, Robert Hickey, our art director, Laurie Tag of subsidiary rights, Sandy Trupp in promotion, Jennifer Prost, and Christopher Jones.

Illustrations were done by Virginia Casey of Little Compton, R.I., with the exception of the accessory illustrations, which were done by Cynthia Neides of Providence, R.I. And thanks to Harry Halliwell of Boston for the cover photo.

Special thanks to Madeleine Stein Wessel.

Extra
Edge

Contents

Part I

A New Look
At Success

x

Chapter 1

The New Executive Woman

If you're an executive woman with the business savvy and talent for a top management position, this book is for you. It is not another warmed-over male 'success book' modified for women. And it's not for the reticent woman who shuns the spotlight, because that is exactly where it's going to put you. It's for the New Executive Woman who has her sights on the very top of her profession. If you are that woman, then you're going to learn about a career factor that successful executives have long known and jealously guarded.

Have you ever wondered what it is that sets one very successful manager apart from other apparently equally qualified candidates for a key position? Maybe you attributed it to hard work! Well, it's a nice idea—that hard work pays off. But we all know business people who devote every hour to the company and never get anywhere. Or maybe you believe luck is the answer. Perhaps, but most executives I know make their own luck. So what, then, is the answer?

When I meet with people in positions of power, I see that they all have one thing in common, something special. It's called Total Professional Style. And if you are going to compete with men for those too-few top positions, then you are going to have to develop it as well. And that is what this book is about.

Total Professional Style

Professional Style is more than the result of a person's clothes—it involves grooming, physical presence, posture, and manner. It's the unmistakable confidence that comes from knowing how to handle any situation. It's an aura of vitality and energy. The executive who has it commands attention at meetings, speaks with confidence and authority, and moves with self-assurance through the corporate corridors.

This is not a "dress for success" book. Developing your own Total Professional Style involves a lot more than putting on a conservative blue suit. In fact, I'll show you later why this could have a negative impact on your career. And don't believe those who tell you to imitate men. It's too simplistic and ultimately self-defeating to apply the principles that work for a man's image to that of a woman. What's needed is a guide designed for women—by an executive woman. That's why this book is unique.

Who Is The New Executive Woman?

Alix,* recently promoted to vice president of a Wall Street investment banking firm, typifies the New Executive Woman. A graduate of the Harvard Business School, Alix is attractive, slim, and feminine. Her dress, hair, and makeup reflect a style and elegance befitting her position. On a typical day, she will chair a departmental meeting, host an important client for lunch at an exclusive French restaurant, and meet with the senior partner of the firm to plot strategies for a billion-dollar corporate merger. In all of these activities she exudes a winning air.

Alix has an excellent chance to become the first senior woman executive in her firm. Part of the reason is that for the first time in history, many of the barriers to women in business and other professions have been reduced. She also has more education and business expertise than her predecessors. There is, however, more to success than doing a good job. Alix knows that the work she does is only a part of being successful—projecting the "right image" is, in fact, fundamental. And in today's highly competitive environment, the New Executive Woman knows it's becoming increasingly important.

"The Extra Edge" . . .

"Image", "class", "finesse" or "style"—it has many names—is the missing ingredient in many women's careers, an ingredient that often decisively makes the differ-

---

*All of the women in this book are real. To ensure their privacy, and to encourage their unreserved participation in the project, we have guaranteed their confidentiality.

ence between winning and losing. It's the "extra edge" that makes the sharp business manager move faster and go farther. In the old days, one might say that it was what separated "the men from the boys." But women are in the game now and in many respects the right image is even more important for them than for their male counterparts.

At one of my recent seminars, a young woman spoke out to say that judging a person by her image was superficial. Fortunately, by the end of the program she realized that nothing could be further from the truth! Image is more than just a veneer or a facade. It's a necessary and complex part of the total package of the successful businesswoman on the move. It serves as a cornerstone of confidence and self-assurance in everything she does. I cannot emphasize enough that developing your own Total Professional Style is something that should not be ignored or left to chance.

A Costly Mistake!

The task is a complex one for women. While the young male executive has many examples to emulate, there are few female executive role models. Most businesswomen are in entry-level positions or in lower middle management. They have been forced to develop their own image and sense of style on the basis of intuition, guesswork, and a lot of luck. Many times they make serious errors.

Melissa had worked very hard as an assistant account executive for a major New York advertising agency. She came in early and was usually the last to leave the office. None of her peers could equal the quality or quantity of her reports. Melissa's efforts resulted in a promotion to account executive on one of the agency's major brands. In her new position she focused her efforts on producing even more reports and memos.

Unfortunately Melissa never paid very much attention to her image. In fact, she felt self-conscious about the way she looked and handled herself, and tended to keep a low profile at the office, especially at meetings with the agency's clients. Her lack of style not only affected the way she thought about herself, but also influenced the way others perceived her. Again and again she failed in the critical role of acting as a buffer between the agency's creative talent and the clients because no one gave her quite the respect she needed to be truly effective. Within a year, Melissa was reassigned to one of the agency's low-priority projects.

Though technically competent, Melissa failed because she projected the wrong image and was unable to influence the right people. On a deeper level, her lack of style formed the basis for a sense of inferiority that adversely influenced her entire job performance. Subconsciously, she felt she simply did not measure up to others around her. Later she spoke candidly of her experiences. "When I looked at the other people at work, they seemed so confident, so sure of themselves. They had a way of making you think they were right, even when I knew for certain they were dead wrong. Yet I was often too intimidated to correct them." Against such odds, all of her efforts were unable to compensate for her underlying deficiencies.

Melissa had to learn the hard way, but at least she finally did. The stakes in business are high, and today's executive woman is now vying against other women, in addition to men, for the "plum" jobs. The savvy and ambitious businesswoman of the '80's must realize that in the Corporate Game, the look of success breeds success.

The Pitfalls of "Expert" Advice

It sometimes seems as though there are more "experts" in the world than information seekers. To a woman developing her professional image and style there are a multitude of people ready to give her advice, from the woman at the cosmetics counter to the salesclerk at her local boutique.

Whenever someone offers you advice for the Executive Suite, consider the following: If that person has no connection with business or is unfamiliar with the specific needs of a woman in business, then you could be headed for a professional "imaging disaster." Many people who make a living out of giving advice to women promote their own ideas about what is "right," to the detriment of the unwary. Unfortunately, all too often their ideas are at odds with business in general, or specific industries in particular. Your image is too important an element of success to be developed on anything but sound and knowledgeable advice.

A Challenge . . .

Are you a woman on the move? Are you ready to stand out from the crowd (in a positive way, of course)? Have you checked out the CEO's office and decided that it needed "a woman's touch"—namely yours? If you answered yes to these questions, then *The Extra Edge* is for you!

Chapter 2

Women and Corporate Success:
Making It In the '80's

Women entering the business world have had to fight many stereotypes. The original "career gal" stereotype formed in the 1940's was personified on screen by such women as Katharine Hepburn and Rosalind Russell. She was severe-looking, wore no makeup, and usually had horn-rimmed glasses perched on the end of her nose. Typically, she was single and had no "beaux." Her movies ended when she let her hair down to become a "real woman" and got her man, or when she opted for her career and lost the man she loved.

The moral was clear—femininity and business don't mix. This lesson was not lost on the next generation of women who entered the business world. Masculinity was good, while femininity a distinct negative. The stage was set for the all-pervasive defeminization of the American businesswoman that came into full swing in the late '70's.

The Macho Woman
Since the businesswoman wants to succeed in a "man's" world, so the logic goes, she should emulate him. Proponents of this theory advocate that the surest way to

succeed is to look and act like a man—women should dress in masculine suits of dark gray or dark blue, and talk tough (to paraphrase John Wayne: "a woman's gotta do what a woman's gotta do . . ."). When these women put on the "business suit," they took off their makeup, jewelry, and any accessories that had a feminine touch. And, in fact, the more masculine the image, some thought, the better.

The Cloning of The American Businesswoman

Probably no one has had a greater effect on this masculinization trend than dress consultants such as John Molloy. During the '70's he wrote a dress for success book for men in which he outlined the unspoken dress code that had existed for years in industry.

He didn't stop there, however, and soon began to issue advice for women. Unfortunately, the look that gave men a sense of style and class did not have the same result for women. By treating all signs of femininity as a negative in business, he effectively eliminated women's individuality as well. The result: imitative versions of the male executive.

Such advice perpetuates the indoctrination that every woman has undergone since childhood—that being a woman is just not good enough—she has to be more like a man if she wants to be successful. Following the "uniform" theory to its logical conclusion, it will be virtually impossible to tell one woman in her blue suit from another in her blue suit. These consultants would turn businesswomen into an army of clones!

The Last Hurrah of The Grey Flannel Suit— (let's hope so, anyway)

Let's face it—the uniform is safe. Women are still getting accustomed to their new role in business, and to many it provides a sense of security. Take Janet, a group product manager of a major consumer goods company: "When I began my career I was so nervous about fitting in that I followed Molloy's book in every detail. If the shoes that I liked weren't in it, I wouldn't wear them. As I became more confident, I began to break away from the mold. After all, I had a lot to offer this company and I wanted to be noticed."

Janet's feelings represent those of a growing number of successful women who disagree with the advice of those consultants whose nondescript uniform makes a woman blend into the woodwork. That's fine if you don't want to be noticed in the company. But dead weight if you want to get to the top!

The Making of an Image

What is your image? Quite simply, it is the sum total of the parts that you present to the world. On its more basic level, (and the way that most people consider its meaning) it is the way you look—your dress, hair, makeup, and overall physique. But also, it's your day-to-day business style—how you communicate your ideas, your "performance" at meetings, how you create visibility, and your command of "corporate finesse." And on a more subtle level, it's how you handle a variety of challenging situations that executives face—office politics, business entertaining and travel, and interviewing for new jobs and promotions.

If you master all of these areas, you have a strong chance of career success, because as far as the rest of the world is concerned, you are your image. And no matter how competent or intelligent a person you are inside, your success in the business world will depend on what is perceived on the outside.

Why Hard Work Alone Is Never The Answer

If you reject the importance of your image, and plan to demonstrate your corporate value by working even harder, you're making a mistake. Regardless of how we may pride ourselves on being rational, logical, and thoughtful human beings, the truth is that everyone forms judgments on people in a matter of seconds—not thoughtfully over a period of time. And fortunately or unfortunately, as the case may be, that split-second judgment is very difficult, sometimes impossible, to change.

According to psychological studies, even experienced personnel executives make strong and immediate judgments using only stereotyped information. On this basis people who are attractive, people with style who project the correct image, get jobs easier and are promoted faster. In other words, the people who make it are those with Total Professional Style.

Welcome To The Real World

There is a good reason why many people, especially women, are dismayed by this cynical view of the "real world." Growing up in the American educational system, we have been programmed to believe that we will be judged in all we do by the fair and impartial standards of the authority figures in our lives.

If we get the same grade in our exams in high school as the boy next to us, or the girl in the first row, we expect approximately the same grade in the course. Such egalitarian standards do not exist in the business world. The corporation has its own set of rules which, more often than not, rewards men and penalizes women.

This is strikingly illustrated by the case of the "anonymous memo." A group of executives were asked to evaluate a project and were told it had been done by a woman. Later they were asked to evaluate the same work, (which was slightly disguised), this time being told that the work had been done by a man. The evaluations of the "man's work" were much higher than those for the work attributed to a woman. The executives assigned so-called "feminine traits" to the work done by the woman—it was "illogical," "not factual," and "difficult" to implement. When considering the identical work supposedly done by a man, however, the comments contained positive and traditional male qualities, such as "coherent," "concise," and "realistic."

Given this overwhelming male-female dichotomy, it is not at all surprising that there has been a great trend toward the masculinization of the American businesswoman in the way she looks, dresses, and acts. After all, it's human nature to gravitate toward behavior that is "rewarded," and away from behavior that is "punished." But this can create a whole new set of problems for today's businesswoman.

Why Can't A Woman Be More Like A Man?

Since women have entered this relatively new environment, (the corporation), many have adopted the maxim "if you can't beat 'em, join 'em." At first, this seems to be the smart thing to do. But as we probe deeper, we begin to see that this is merely a stop-gap measure. By emulating masculine images, rather than working to create their own, these women are following an approach that will not serve them effectively through the next few decades of corporate life. And, it can actually backfire.

The Need For Individuality

With the advent of the prefabricated business uniform for women, individuality and personal style were stifled. Formula dressing eliminated any possibility for a woman to express her uniqueness while she demonstrated her professionalism. At the same time, career advancement was becoming enormously competitive. Individuality and the ability to attract attention favorably are distinct advantages in the climb to the top.

Just as important is the psychological factor. Harvard's Kathy Fox, a career counselor who advises middle management women, says, "It's vital to a woman's success to express her individuality. When she makes that psychological 'jump' into her own true identity, rather than imitating her peers, her career enters a new, much more successful phase."

Extra
Edge

17

Sooner or later, women must realize that one of their biggest advantages is natural visibility. Yet so many women today are casting this aside and melting into the group. And what do you think all the men are doing in the meantime?—they're trying to distinguish themselves from one another so that they can step into the spotlight!

It is becoming abundantly clear that in the long run the women who will be successful are those who manage to develop their own unique style and image. Those who develop Total Professional Style will draw upon their special strengths as women while recognizing the realities of the male-dominated world.

Chapter 3

The Harvard Interviews
Part I:
A New Look at Success

What do today's successful businesswomen think about career success in the '80's? What are the success factors that are important to them? As their role in business grows, what strategies are today's women developing to continue the momentum?

Researching the "Science of Success"

These can be awesome questions and the answers can be quantitatively researched to a 99 percent probability. Or they can be presented in some esoteric correlation between the number of hairs on a subject's head and her chances of success. But often the numbers and statistics don't tell the whole story. Too often the respondents surveyed are subconsciously influenced by the formality of the studies, or respond with answers that they think sound important and responsible. Instead, in our research I wanted to explore these important issues with successful women in straightforward, "no-holds-barred" interviews.

When I first became interested in the subject of women and career success, my co-author, a Harvard graduate, recommended that we use women graduates of the

Harvard Business School as the subjects of our studies. He pointed out that this would assure that all the respondents had similar credentials and comparable degrees of intelligence and ambition. Consequently, we could focus exclusively on the more subtle aspects of career success.

Why Harvard Graduates Make It— "The West Point of Capitalism"

This was not the only reason for selecting Harvard Business School women graduates, however. Harvard is a "generalist" business school. Its curriculum emphasizes many different aspects of business, especially the subtle interpersonal side of the corporate world, instead of concentrating solely on technical skills as many business schools do.

Much of this orientation is due to the use of the "case method," an approach in which students are presented with a detailed and real company problem in a 30 to 40 page detailed report, or "case." On the basis of this information, they must define the problems and develop solutions. But most interestingly, all of this takes place in an open-forum type of atmosphere where everyone is expected to contribute. The professor merely guides the discussion. And from an individual's point of view, how a student presents his/her ideas is usually more important than the specifics of their comments. This is because at the Harvard Business School, like the real world, style and presentation really count.

As a result of this education, the HBS graduate is ready to shoot for corporate success immediately. They are already accustomed to constant comparison with their peers in an open, competitive atmosphere. They are keenly attuned to the more subtle aspects of business: interpersonal behavior, navigating the "structure within the corporate structure," and effectively presenting a positive image to others. It is small wonder, then, that there are far more HBS graduates at the head of U.S. corporations than from any other school. And why the Harvard Business School is known world-wide as the "West Point of Capitalism."

The Women in our Studies

We confined our studies to women who had graduated from HBS within the last 15 years, since the late '60's marked the first noticeable increase in the number of women in graduate business schools and in professional business positions. The women were all told to assume that their educational credentials, their job performance, and their ambition were roughly comparable to those of their business peers. To get the most honest and realistic answers, we assured their anonymity. We then asked the women a series of questions pertaining to image, professional style, career success, success strategies, and what it takes to make it in their companies and industries.

The results of these interviews serve as a foundation for most of the philosophies presented here. They also are the source of the many real life stories of career "success and failure" presented throughout.

Image—A Major Success Factor

HARVARD STUDY QUESTION

How important has your "image" been in your career progress to date?

Most of the women interviewed, 75 percent, felt strongly that their image was an "important" or "very important" factor in their success, and would continue to be, even at top management levels. Many felt that the "right image" had played a major role in getting their first job and in their subsequent promotions. They also shared the opinion that people attributed more positive qualities to them because of their images, regardless of their actual abilities. And most importantly, these women believed that their professional image had helped them to gain quick acceptance by the men in their corporation. On the other side, only 8 percent thought that image was of no importance to their career.

One consultant summed it up as follows: "Image is everything in business, especially in my business. If the client doesn't have faith in you, he's not going to accept your proposals, regardless of your credentials. Of course, the reputation of my company precedes me, but when I walk in that door to meet the CEO of a company, I've got two minutes to make a good impression. I'd better look and act as if I can handle the job."

Looking Good Gets Results

What are the important elements of today's New Executive Woman's image?

Extra
Edge

HARVARD STUDY QUESTION

How important is "looking good" (dressing well, making the most of your looks with appropriate makeup, wearing flattering yet professional-looking hairstyling) to your image as a professional?

Sixty-nine percent of the women polled felt that looking attractive, (as well as professional) was a definite plus. It was not too long ago that professional women feared that looking attractive would make them appear unprofessional. Fortunately, the trend today is toward the woman who has it all—looks, brains, and power!

As one women lawyer at a top firm put it: "It gives me an added advantage, particularly over men—and I'm going to use it." Interestingly, women in the so-called "people-oriented" fields placed even more emphasis on good looks.

The End of an Era—The "Uniform" Era

HARVARD STUDY QUESTION

How important a part of your wardrobe is the so-called "Molloy uniform?"* What does or did it mean to you?

*THE UNIFORM—the Molloy look: dark two-button blazer, matching A-line skirt, man-tailored white blouse, clear tan stockings, dark pumps.

The majority (65 percent) of the women were putting their "business uniforms" to rest as obsolete, or were "seriously considering" doing so. They no longer felt that wearing the strict uniform, (instead of other more stylish but professional-looking suits and dresses), contributed to their professional image. Most (66 percent) said that they had worn the uniform originally because they didn't know what else to wear and they were afraid of making a mistake in their professional appearance.

Jean, a marketing director for a consumer products company: "Things are different now than when Molloy first wrote his book. A lot has changed—especially in the types of clothing for women who want to look professional but who don't want to be confined to one look. When I started in business, there really weren't many clothes that were appropriate for me as a businesswoman. Now there are so many that I'm constantly buying new suits and dresses. And I feel great about the way I look, and the way I feel about myself."

HARVARD STUDY QUESTION

Only for women who have worked more than five years in professional positions: Do you feel more comfortable now in deviating from the uniform than you did when you first started your job?

This question evoked resounding (78 percent) agreement. It was apparent that the more successful a woman is, the more secure she feels in turning away from the prefabricated look of the last decade.

This seemed to be a standard pattern among most of the women. For their first job, they wore the "uniform." As they became more familiar with the company and business in general, they began loosening up the uniform formula. At the time of their first promotion, they began looking for suits and dresses that showed they were definitely on the way up. One financial manager who now heads a department with five subordinates at the executive headquarters of a New York conglomerate told me that "I really can't believe I ever used to wear the uniform constantly, it's so uninspiring! Now, I wear suits, coordinates, and dresses—whatever my mood is."

Extra
Edge

23

HARVARD STUDY QUESTION

How important is your own personal sense of individuality to the way you choose to look and dress on the job? And how important do you think it will be to your ultimate career success?

The affirmative response in 81 percent of the answers confirmed that their sense of individuality was an extremely important factor in the degree of success these Harvard graduates felt they would achieve. Many were looking for more ways to establish their own identity while staying within the corporate structure. Some expressed a very real fear of becoming one of hundreds of indistinguishable "white collar" workers in a vast corporation.

Appearance on the job was frequently cited as the first place to start in developing and maintaining a sense of individuality. A certain hairstyle, a unique accessory, an unusual suit were all mentioned as examples of "personal" touches. One New York marketing analyst stated, "I'll never give up suits altogether, but I'm really excited by the new look in suits. I can still look professional but now I feel as if I have my personal stamp on my looks."

Femininity * *Is Back—In Force*

* **THE NEW EXECUTIVE WOMAN'S DEFINITION OF FEMININITY** refers to a woman who is comfortable and proud of her womanhood. A woman who is attractive AND professional. Femininity is no longer a synonym for weak, helpless, flirtatious, scatterbrained, or any other perjorative term sometimes previously associated with the word.

HARVARD STUDY QUESTION

Is femininity (as an element of your Professional Image) good or bad for your career? Have you considered "feminizing" your image on the job?

This definition of the word "femininity" was the basis for the question. Virtually all of the respondents acknowledged the difference between the word's new and old meanings, rejecting many such traditional synonyms as soft, vulnerable, weak, and helpless. Being assured that by femininity we meant "a self-assured, confident acknowledgment that one is a woman," 61 percent of the women interviewed stated that they were "feminizing" their image. And they were doing it because it was good for their careers and personal self images.

Fitness and Personal Image

HARVARD STUDY QUESTION

How important is a woman's physical condition as a career factor?

Seventy percent of the respondents said that a woman's physical condition was "somewhat important" or "very important" as a career factor. One Wall Street investment banker had this to say: "I think being in shape and looking slim are important to anyone's image. It's all part of your self-confidence—if you know you look good, you just naturally feel better about yourself. And that shows up in a number of different ways—how you act, how you relate to others, how you handle yourself in a business discussion. The reverse is also true. If you're overweight or your clothes make you look heavy or flabby, you feel more self-conscious. You try to hide, to avoid attention. You're not going to get ahead that way."

A professional's image entails a lot more than just the right clothes. And it starts with the condition that your body is in. Our society

Extra
Edge

places great emphasis on looks, physical fitness, and body shape in all aspects of our everyday life, and on the job is no exception. Even in the political arena, the overweight cigar-smoking "boss" has largely been replaced by trim, fit politicians. The same is true in business, for both men and women. You have to look slim and healthy and be energetic. That's part of a winning style.

Executive "Finesse"

In many of our interviews we got the feeling that there's a growing understanding by businesswomen of the importance of personal style and sophistication in the Corporate World of the '80's. It is apparent that doing a good job is no longer enough. You've got to have something extra.

Perhaps this is because there are so many highly qualified individuals competing for limited positions. Or because our society is becoming increasingly "class" conscious and places a high degree of respect on those individuals who convey a sense of style, who seem to be comfortable in any social situation, and who always seem to know the right thing to say and do. Manners, upbringing, style, executive finesse—whatever you call it—is a hot property for executives right now.

An investment banker with a very blue-blooded firm said, "An important part of my job is interacting with people of wealth, stature, and influence, mostly outside of the office. So of course I have to know how to handle myself socially. But even if I didn't interact as much, handling myself in those non-office business situations would still be important to my career."

Chapter 4

The
Harvard
Interviews
Part II:
Success Strategies
for Different Industries

Success in business is a complex subject. And it's very difficult to get good advice, because there is so much bad advice out there. To make matters worse, strategies that may work very well in one industry could be disastrous in another. Each industry has its own environment. And if you're to be successful, it's essential that you adopt strategies that work in your industry's "corporate culture."

This book is all about developing a professional style that has the best chance of engendering success. It covers all aspects of executive style—from how to dress and walk, to how to handle interpersonal behavior and executive entertaining. In other words, it's a guide to a Total Professional Style which will serve as the foundation for your future success in business. And to developing a success style that is in tune with your work environment.

Extra
Edge

The Competitive Advantage

Many people have significant talents and skills. And if talent and skill alone were the sole determinants of achievement, those individuals would be successful in any number of fields. But career success is not that simple, and the most successful people are those who selected, (intentionally or otherwise), fields in which they have some natural, "competitive advantage." In other words, careers in which their professional style and abilities are appreciated and rewarded.

Most career books only tell you what the particular responsibilities of a specific field are, or which credentials are required for entry positions. Or they may present massive survey results showing that the chief executive officers of such-and-such an industry average 5'11" in height, went to east coast schools, and have 2.1 children. Alternately, you can find "image consultants" who have never worked in a major corporation advising that to be successful in a particular career you should wear the "uniform", or some other prefabricated outfit.

These approaches to understanding career success are too simplistic and are ultimately of little value. Of course, you need certain skills and credentials for specific careers, and obviously it's best to dress appropriately for your industry, but these are only part of a larger requirement of career success. Your best chances of "making it" comes when there is a match of your overall style and temperament with the "success requirements" of your industry.

In our interviews, we asked some women graduates of the Harvard Business School to define the elements of style that generate career success in their fields.

HARVARD STUDY QUESTION

> Do you think that the requirements for success are fairly uniform from industry to industry? Or are there special characteristics required to really "make it" in each?

Only 15 percent thought that the requirements for success were uniform from industry to industry. Eighty percent believed that the mix of skills, talents, and image required for success varied considerably from industry to industry, while five percent were not sure.

As you will see, different fields have their own atmosphere, their own pace and style. If your style "fits," if success in that field requires the talents and image which you possess, then your chances of long term success are greatly enhanced. If not, you could spend your career life beating your head up against the proverbial brick wall.

In our interviews we explored the differences in different industries in order to develop a success "profile" for a number of careers. We discussed the requirements for success and what constituted a "success style" in each. In other words we wanted to learn what characteristics successful individuals in those fields have in common.

The results presented are not meant to define rigid "success formulas." Instead, they are offered to give you a feel for what it takes to "make it" in these fields. You must observe your industry, your company, and your specific situation in order to refine our general descriptions.

What Successful Harvard Women Say About Their Industries

Marketing/Brand Management

Brand management in many ways is like being the owner of your own company. And all of it revolves around one brand, or product. It might be Tide detergent, Maxwell House coffee, or Frosted Flakes.

Most of the women in this field felt that you had to be entrepreneurially inclined to succeed. You have to have strong personal power and be politically savvy. As a brand manager, you oversee all the elements of a product and work with many different departments—sales, packaging, promotion, manufacturing, research & development, and advertising.

Yet, though you control the entire process, from manufacturing to the final sales, in reality you have no "real" power over any of these staff group personnel. They report to their own superiors, and work on many different brands. Yet, their cooperation is vital to your performance. As such, your ultimate success or failure depends to a great extent on your ability to motivate others subtly, and over a long period of time without "wearing out" your relationships.

You have to be a "jack of all trades, master of none." You must understand and coordinate everything that happens to your product, and you sign-off on all the work done in connection with it. So if there is a foul-up in the packaging artwork, or the sales promotion is delayed, or the agency wasn't notified about the consumer test, you are held responsible, even though the mistake was not your own.

This is where being politically savvy can get you results. If you have the right contacts within the company, if you know when to call in favors, if you build a strong power base, you'll get things done. If you try to play it alone, or play "hard ball," you're finished. This is one business in which you can't be a loner or a tough guy.

Sales

People in sales have diverse backgrounds since there are no specific credentials that are required and many companies have their own training programs. The "sales" career varies with the company and the product you sell. As a salesperson you can find yourself selling high ticket and sophisticated products such as computer hardware, industrial equipment, or commercial real estate. Or you could be making the rounds of food and drug stores promoting your company's health and beauty aid line. But regardless of the product, there are strong similarities in all selling careers. And if you are really good you can make fantastic salaries.

While the entry requirements may not be as formidable as in other fields, selling is not for everyone. In fact it takes a special combination of traits to be successful. Many people with otherwise impressive credentials have failed completely in this field. According to one woman with a multi-national company, "I see people all the time with graduate degrees who think that their education and intelligence alone guarantee success. But the only thing that counts in sales is how much you sell."

Self-discipline is also important. In the "field," there's no one watching over you, giving you that impetus to keep going. It's all up to you. As one sales manager for an office products company put it, "It's easy to be motivated in the beginning. You're excited about your product and your new job. But after a while, the novelty wears off. Because you work out in the field, you know that you can get up a little later, or finish a little earlier, and it's tempting because no one will know. But you can't, because once you start chipping away at your schedule and lose the discipline of your day, you're in trouble. You have to be as structured as if you had a desk two feet away from your boss. No, even more so!"

The biggest problem most people have in sales is rejection, coupled with the innate uncertainty of the selling process. The most successful salespeople see rejection as a challenge and never take it personally. One woman who sells industrial equipment suggested, "See selling as a percentages game. Never expect to sell on every call. Instead, look upon success as one sale in every five or ten prospects. Then when you have nine rejections and one sale, you'll feel like a winner. And even though you may not sell today, you must have confidence that over a period of time you'll make your quota."

Commercial Banking

This is the "gentlemen's" business, which is now also becoming the "gentlewomen's" business. The atmosphere, in contrast to that of some others, is sedate, formal, and civilized. Manners, impeccable taste in clothing, appearance, and behavior are necessities. You cannot afford to commit a social gaffe or wear declassé clothing. If you can appear conservatively elegant, you're on your way. Subtlety of style is very important.

Good credentials, a college degree from a respectable school, and an acceptable appearance can get you in the running for one of the training programs. But the competition is getting tougher each year as more people, unable or unwilling to go to graduate business schools, opt for bank training programs.

If you have an MBA or want to go where the real action is, chances are you're better off in the commercial lending section. There is more competition in this area, and the candidates have strong credentials. But you have to be willing to take risks here. Contrary to popular belief, a sharp lending officer will have loan defaults as well as successes in her portfolio. As a loan officer from a major banking institution pointed out, "Every loan has some degree of risk. If you only approve those loans that are virtually guaranteed to be paid back, then you're too conservative and you can be losing new clients and money for the bank. You have to take some risks."

If you are ambitious, you should hide it beneath a veneer of quiet reserve. Blatant ambition, which is encouraged in other fields, is out of place in this world.

Stock Brokerage

Credentials aren't as important in this field as in others. But that's primarily because this is one of the few positions where you are accountable for the bottom line from the start. If you bring in lots of money, you stay. If you can't, you go. And usually pretty quickly.

Extra
Edge

Most of the women interviewed in this field felt that you have to be supremely self-motivating and self-confident to make it as a female stockbroker. You also have to have a "thick skin" because you are going to be rejected far more often than you're accepted when prospecting for business. In many respects, you're an independent businesswoman who is responsible for managing your "company," (your portfolio of clients), successfully. Your firm is there essentially to provide you with an office, a telephone, and a secretary. The rest is up to you. There's a great deal of latitude if you are good, and lucrative salaries at a young age are not uncommon.

Some of the women felt very strongly about the importance of their image in this business. As one woman put it, "You've got to give your clients the impression that you've made money and you can help them make money, too. Who wants a poor stockbroker to handle their hard-earned cash? You have to let the clients think you know how to make money for them—even if you make more money for yourself on a trade than you do for them."

You have to be decisive and fast-acting. Opportunities aren't going to sit around waiting for you to make up your mind. Once you have a deal you have to know which clients to call and how to get them to act quickly. One of the women said, "It takes a lot of psychology—knowing what to say to people to make them give you their money. When I meet with my clients or entertain them for lunch or dinner, I play a role. If my client likes fast action and lots of risk, I let him think I'm a high roller too. That's when I bring out the heavy artillery clothes—my fur, my diamonds, everything that says I'm in the money. If my client is ultra-conservative, then I'm the model of cautious optimism."

Retailing

Retailing is a hectic, hard-paced industry with a mix of drudgery and glamour. The typical path to top management is via the "buyer" route. The career of a buyer usually connotes a "jet-set" world of European fashion houses, haute couture and world-renowned designers. While this can be a part of the buyer's life, the reality is less glitter and much more hard work.

At the entry level, the future buyer is assigned to a specific department within the store. It's almost invariably the least exciting area and responsibilities involve assisting the manager of the department—which can mean anything from dusting the shelves, to rearranging displays, or handling unpleasant customers. The hours are long and initially unrewarding. But it's the price that must be paid before the buyer can move on to the more exciting departments. The trainee must become an expert in each department—knowing the suppliers, the product, the customer, and in general how to manage it.

As in many other fields, the buyer has to have confidence in her decisions. Contrary to appearances, her decisions are based on a lot more than sheer intuition. A successful buyer has her finger on the pulse of the retailing world. She watches carefully to spot trends—one year the Italians may exert a major influence on the ready-to-wear, the next the Japanese designers may be popular. The fashion writers and the designers' publicists may be predicting a new fashion—but that doesn't always make her customers buy. In the end, she has to know what will sell. Buying a huge inventory of a design that flops can be costly to her career plans.

A strong sense of personal style is necessary in retailing, particularly the fashion area. A successful buyer has to continually demonstrate her own creativity and cachet in everything she wears and does. If she doesn't make herself look good, how is she going to establish an identity for her department or store? "Whenever I tell people I'm a buyer, I can see them mentally assessing how I look, down to the tiniest detail of my clothing. They expect me to look special and if I don't they will think that I'm not successful. Even when I'm out for a stroll, I have to look casual chic. But actually, I love the business so much that I enjoy experimenting with different looks," was the way one woman described it.

Accounting

If you want to make it in the Big Eight accounting firms, you have to have a blend of concern for detail, facility with numbers, and a desire for precision, all balanced by an outgoing personality. You need to be someone who fits in well with many different kinds of people. The old stereotype of the accountant, (dull, dry, a loner more interested in numbers than people), has changed remarkably, especially in the top firms.

More and more accountants are being pushed out into the world. As one accountant with a Big Eight firm told us, "I love the challenge of putting all the pieces of the financial puzzle together. That's why I chose accounting. I never expected to join an accounting firm and see the world—and yet I've been to Europe an average of twice a year for the last eight years."

If you want the rewards of an accounting career (and there are many, including a partnership with a lucrative salary), you have to be willing to cope with the entry

Extra
Edge

level "drudge-work." You have to be cooperative, accept assignments which may be extremely tedious, and be patient—to "pay your dues" while working hard to move up. "You can complain throughout your entire training period, or you can grin and bear it. If you keep a smile on your face and a good attitude, it really pays off well," according to another accountant.

Advertising

There are two key areas in advertising, but many people mistakenly think that the typical agency person is epitomized by a wildly creative, independent eccentric. To set the record straight, these characteristics are from the creative department. The "creative's" counterpart at the agency is the "account executive"—generally much more conservative, more the company person, who serves as the go-between for the creative department and the client. Each career requires vastly different talents and styles.

The Creative Side

If you get into the creative side of the agency, where they write the copy and conjure up the images for the advertisements, you need the talent to come up with ideas that make the old seem new. In a few words or pictures you've got to excite people, motivate them, and make them do something they would not ordinarily do. And you need to have your fingertips on the pulse of the "masses."

If that is your forte you can go a long way in advertising. As a "creative," you also have far fewer requirements to conform to—in a sense, you can get away with behavior that would get you canned in another industry. As the head copywriter for a "hot shot" agency put it, "People expect me to look different—they have in their minds the idea that a creative person should wear unusual clothes and act slightly temperamental and strange. If I met the client in a conservative grey suit and acted like a typical corporate manager they would be disappointed. They'd wonder whether I was really creative."

The creative side is a hectic, harried, tough arena. You can appear to be an "artist," in fact you may be an artist, but you can't be too temperamental or overly sensitive. One woman had this to say, "Regardless of how we look or act or whether we deal in ideas or artwork, in the end we are a business and a tough one. If I took personally every rejection of my copy, I would have shot myself years ago. You just take the rejection, go back to the desk and come up with another idea."

The Account Side

This is the side most people forget when they think of advertising. The account executives, the people who interface on almost a daily basis with the client, are the flip side of the creatives. The account people look like business people, they dress in typical corporate style, they act "normal," and they try very hard to keep the client happy. They are the conduits between the creatives and the clients. They hold the client's hand and let them know that they will keep a "rein" on the creatives so that they don't go overboard. And they massage the egos of the creatives. The account people are very similar to the brand managers in marketing, with whom they often work, and the positions share many of the same "success requirements."

Just as brand people have to oversee a variety of departments to keep the brand going, the account person has to oversee a variety of departments within the agency—the creatives, the researchers, the media people, and the accountants. But unlike the brand person who only has to please the people in her company, the account person has to please the people in her company and those in the client company. For the account person, that can mean a lot of flak from all sides.

Consequently, an account person has to have strong social skills and generate a strong sense of personal power and respect. Otherwise they can be trampled. One woman put it this way: "I have to interpret what brand people want, when they may not even know what they want. Then I have to decide whether we're on the right track. If we are, I have to then make sure the creatives know what the client wants and get them to produce it. Of course, half the time after I do this, I get that wonderful phone call from the client saying they've changed their minds. And the creatives get on my back. But I love it, I thrive on the pressure, the deadlines, the frantic scrambling from agency to client to the location of the commercial shoot."

Another area in which the account executives need to excel is in business entertaining, of which there is a considerable amount. They have to know how to keep the client pleased with the agency and lots of times this is done over dinner or lunch. It's all part of the personal touch, the "soft sell," that keeps things moving.

Law

While there are many different types of legal positions, we explored the in-house corporate lawyer, who advises on everything from the legal ramifications of a merger to the use of a trademark on a product. In most companies the lawyers do their work "behind the scenes." Walk into an ad agency, and there may be a battery of lawyers working on the legality of the agency's numerous ads, but they rarely are a high visibility employee. In fact, in many companies, the legal department is quietly ensconced in its own subdued domain, far away from the madding crowd.

If you want to make business law your career you have to be willing to sacrifice much of your personal life. As one corporate lawyer for a marketing company put it, "In the beginning, you do a lot of routine, boring and detailed work during the day and then you bring home a lot more routine, boring and detailed work. I usually have ten or fifteen different legal questions I'm working on at one time And I'm always being interrupted by a frantic marketing manager who has to have the answer to a new problem immediately. I may stay up all night working out the problem so that the manager can display his ability for getting things done. But that's law—there's no quick or easy way to approach the problem. There's always some new precedent to consider."

A successful corporate lawyer is one who knows business as well as law. Simplistically approaching business situations from a purely legal perspective can have disastrous consequences, including the loss of valuable opportunities. Her advice has to combine what is best from a purely business standpoint with what is best from a purely legal view. A sense of the practical and the expedient is necessary.

The legal department has its own corporate culture which often has no similarity to the culture of the corporation as a whole. Whatever the industry, the law department is usually conservative, cautious, unemotional and sedate. There is little jungle-fighting or brilliant career coups. Career progress is orderly and predictable. According to one of the corporate lawyers with whom we spoke, "At all times, we have to give the impression that we are in control. Cool and unflappable. Even when the brand manager is having a fit right in front of me because I advised against a certain advertising claim, I never lose my reserve. People don't expect lawyers to do anything emotional or thoughtless—and I have to have that image, even if I feel like throwing him out of my office. One quick act could jeopardize my career in this company."

Consulting

Many people, particularly the consultants themselves, like to think that this is where the "crème de la crème" are. Just getting an interview at some of the top companies (McKinsey, Boston Consulting Group, Booz-Allen) requires that you have impeccable credentials. Impeccable usually means solid business experience topped off by a graduate degree at one of the top business schools such as Harvard, Stanford, or Wharton. And, it requires the "right" image—one of style, class, and worldliness.

According to the women with whom we spoke, once you are there, several factors become paramount to your career progress. An ability to handle yourself with ease and competence in a variety of interpersonal situations was often mentioned. (In other words, a strong sense of politics within your own company and the one for which you are consulting). Communication skills are also essential, since you must write effectively and present your findings and recommendations cogently to top managers at both your firm and the client company. A confident and effective presentation will go a long way toward a successful career in consulting.

Appearance, style, and polish were also frequently mentioned. Do you live up to the "hot shot" reputation of your firm? Do you look, act, and dress impeccably? Can you command the respect of those you work with and advise? Said one of the women interviewed: "As a consultant, I may be advising a Silicon Valley sales manager one day, and an oil company senior exec another. I have to establish confidence and a rapport with everyone, immediately."

You need to have dogged determination and energy that will see you through the complexities of each new problem and keep you going, often 'round-the-clock'. As one woman stated, "I haven't spent a weekend at home in the last six months. I'm always hopping a plane to some new location. And sometimes I have to have an initial meeting with a new client after two hours of sleep. But I can't slow down. If I do, I stop. The pace is constant and if you're the type of person who wants to know where you'll be the day after tomorrow, you won't make it. To be successful in this business, you have to sacrifice your personal life to a great degree."

Investment Banking

Again, as with consulting, only the top few from the major business schools get to become members of this elite club. In some sense, you have to be a "gambler" who knows when to play your hunches, and confident enough to take those risks. On the other hand, you need to have a solid grasp of the intricacies of finance, so that you can be attuned to these opportunities. According to one very successful woman: "I'm succeeding because I can practically "smell" a deal. My mind stores all the bits of information floating around me, and suddenly the pieces come together—that's when I know I've got a deal. I'm not really 'smarter' than my associates, everyone here is intelligent, but I'm more intuitive. And I act faster than others."

Extra
Edge

The ability to synthesize information, to ferret out what the information "really" means and then get the point across to other people, is essential. As another investment banker told us, "I'm a good saleswoman, basically. I know what people need to do and I convince them to do it. My job is to make people happy—happy with me and with the deals I make for them."

Like consultants, investment bankers meet with high level executives of client companies on a regular basis. They must be mature, sophisticated, and polished to fulfill their roles.

The Entrepreneur

Courage and a truly independent spirit are two ingredients that the entrepreneur needs. According to one very successful entrepreneur, "My business associates, and even my family, were stunned when I decided to leave the corporate world to start my own business. They couldn't understand why I would want to leave a prestigious job as an advertising executive to start my own business. Quite a few told me that I was throwing my education away. They just didn't understand that I could get more satisfaction building something of my own, putting money directly into my pocket, instead of making a profit for the partners of the agency."

The successful entrepreneur needs a diversity of talents. She must market her product or service, oversee production, in essence manage every area of the business. And then, when the company has grown and is successful, she has to know when to rely on others. The successful entrepreneur works all the time. Perhaps she's not sitting at a desk, but whatever she is doing, part of her mind is always on her business. One entrepreneur's perspective: "I'm always thinking about my business—what can I do to promote it, should I hire a publicist or can I do it myself, when should I expand without jeopardizing my cash flow? I found that even on my nights out socializing, I would eventually turn the conversation around to my business. I could never get this excited about my work at IBM. That was just a job."

Whatever the business, the entrepreneur has to have strong self-confidence. She is usually too far ahead of her associates to count on the opinion of others, and must believe in her own vision. So she needs to be confident enough to follow her instincts, despite an endless barrage of negatives and "can't do's" from everyone around her. That's what makes the successful entrepreneur.

Some entrepreneurs make the mistake of downplaying or ignoring their image once they are on their own. They think that they no longer need a professional look. Nothing could be further from the truth. The image of an entrepreneur is absolutely critical to success. The entrepreneur is selling herself as much as she is selling her product or service. If she looks sloppy or acts unprofessionally, she can destroy the credibility of her business.

Customers, contacts, and potential investors can overlook the fact that she doesn't have an opulent office building for her company. But she herself must look successful and project the image of having the "right stuff." That means she must convey the idea that she's made it and that she doesn't need others, even before she's started. Like the stockbroker, most entrepreneurs find that no one wants to give up their money to them if they think it's really needed. That's why "seed" capital to start new businesses is so difficult to get.

For this reason, the entrepreneur needs to project a very special image. Depending upon what she is trying to do, there is more latitude in the specifics of her image. But one rule must be followed. And that is that she must come across as sophisticated, energetic and vital, and somebody worth dealing with.

Chapter 5

Other Studies On Imaging, Style & Career Success

In our research on the new executive woman and her image, we uncovered some interesting studies. These findings add further emphasis to the fact that first impressions and other imaging considerations are critical to how others see us, and to our ultimate level of career success.

Is Your Career a Short Story?

A number of studies have been done to show that tall men are more successful in business than short men. The same correlation appears to hold true for women. The short woman is at a definite disadvantage. The very fact that she has to look up at most men immediately makes her less threatening and consequently weaker.

According to WATCH* Program research, "small" has historically been equated with a lack of power. And in the business world, power is what it's all about.

If you're over twenty, chances are that you're not going to grow any taller. But there are ways to give the illusion of more height and thus increase your command of attention. In recent years, the retailing industry has taken notice of the "petite" woman and is now making sophisticated clothes for her size. We'll discuss in *Corporate Camouflage* a number of tricks you can use to create the illusion of height. (No, not five inch heels!!).

Are You "Older" Than Your Male Peers—Who Happen To Be The Same Age?

Ah, the inequities—they keep increasing as a woman ages. The greying temples of your male counterpart enhance his image, adding a touch of sophistication and worldliness. For some reason, the same grey color in a woman's hair rarely has the same positive effect. It usually serves only to indicate advancing years.

The craggy lines in his face denote character and strength. They don't do the same for you. Research has shown that the older woman faces greater job discrimination than the older man. And in many instances, greying hair and wrinkles conjure up maternal images.

There is one good thing about grey hair and wrinkles. You don't necessarily have to keep them. With today's cosmetics and surgery, both can be substantially treated. Many of the hair-coloring products on the market not only cover the grey but can help to improve your hair's overall appearance and health. And there have been a number of advances in the treatment of sagging and wrinkling skin.

If you are still young enough not to have either, then begin now to practice preventive measures. Avoid the sun and don't smoke, for starters. And it's not vain or superficial to be concerned. It makes good business sense. Because whether you like it or not, when you're up for a promotion years from now, your wrinkles or grey hair can lose it for you. While no personnel executive wants to admit that these factors can have an effect on their selection of employees, (because it is discriminatory and against the law), a number of them told me off the record that the appearance of age in a woman is a distinctly negative factor, much more so than in a man.

Women Advancing Through Career Help Program, located in New York.

Does Your Boss Inversely Relate Your Bust Size With Your IQ?

We all are familiar with the cliche of the buxom blonde whose IQ is exceeded by her bra size. She's a standard Hollywood character. Unfortunately, new findings have confirmed that many men (and even women) really do associate a large bust with a small brain.

Cambridge, Massachusetts psychologist Chris Kleinke, a researcher in the area of first impressions, conducted a study on character impressions generated by a large bust. His results indicated that women with large busts are judged relatively unintelligent and incompetent. The women with small busts were assumed to be intelligent and competent. The study was conducted using one woman and taking side-view shots of her with her normal bust (small) and two pictures with her bra stuffed to double its size. With each increase, her intelligence and competency ratings dropped.

Susan, a business school graduate with an hourglass figure, wanted a career in consulting. Despite her impeccable credentials, she was turned down by her first-choice firm. A few months later she approached them again, insisting on another try. This time she was hired. It wasn't until much later that she found out that the reason she had been rejected initially was the way she looked. "They took one look at me and no one wanted to believe that I could do the job. They assumed I was a stereotype and didn't bother to look any deeper."

Regardless of how unjust you may find this, you can't escape the facts. If you are large-busted, you have a corporate liability. I'm not suggesting that unless you get a breast reduction you'll be a failure. What I am recommending is that you be cognizant of the negative impressions that can be generated by a large bust and take steps to disguise your bust size. That is not as difficult as it might seem, as I point out in Chapter 9, *Corporate Camouflage.*

Weighty Issues

According to research done by the National Personnel Associates, overweight applicants—both men and women—have more difficulty finding jobs than do their thinner peers. It seems that excess weight connotes laziness and sloppiness in addition to poor physical fitness. To an employer, those characteristics do not signal the best candidate for the job.

In one sense, the employer may be right. The executive in poor physical condition generally has less energy and less stamina to ward off illness. Most top-level positions require long hours, and a low energy level will make it difficult to keep up. Thus overweight people may give the impression of being lazy when they are actually working as hard as their bodies will allow.

We did a quick survey of top-ranking men and women, and found only a handful who could be termed overweight. Most appeared to be in relatively good physical condition. It appears that if you want to make it to the top, your chances are much better if you appear physically fit. We are not advocating that everyone be slim, or even thin. It is obvious that people have different builds and some people are naturally bigger or stockier than others. But you can control your fitness.

Are you solid? Have you turned to flab? Do you exercise regularly to keep muscle tone and build endurance? We know that in the corporate world there are relatively few hours to spare, but there are ways to maintain or increase your physical fitness even at your desk. (*See Chapter 14, The Corporate Body*). We'll also show you how to disguise excess weight and appear slimmer by selecting the right outfit and accessories in *Corporate Camouflage*.

Do You Walk Like a Winner?

You are interviewing for a new job and enter the office and face the personnel executive of your potential employer. Or maybe it's your new boss or a roomful of people waiting for an interdepartmental meeting to begin. Without saying a word, you've already told everyone there how you feel about yourself. And, perhaps more importantly, how they should feel about you.

The way you walk, your posture, your pace, your demeanor, all send signals. When you enter an interview situation do you show immediately that you're intimidated by not standing tall? Do you tell your corporate peers that you're insecure about your ideas by the way you sit at a meeting? Or do you unintentionally convey the idea that you're a lot more interested in picking up a man than you are in picking up a balance sheet when you walk down the corridor?

Professor of kinesiology (the study of movement) Maurita Robarger has observed that your walk can be a barometer of personal moods. According to her research, there are a number of different types of walks. As you become aware of your walk, you can use it or change it, to control the message that you want others to receive. More on walks in *The Corporate Body*.

Chapter 6

What's Your IQ?
(Image Quotient)

Now that we have discussed Total Professional Style and its importance to your career, it's time to get to work developing your own. Before we begin, we have prepared a questionnaire that is meant to start you thinking about the different aspects of your image and your career prospects.

The IQ Test

Part I. Your Career

	Yes	No
1. Do you currently have a management/professional position?	____	
2. Are you interested in advancing to the next level in your career path?	____	

		Yes	No
3.	While you may find that your direction changes from time to time, do you always have some specific career plan in mind anyway?	____	
4.	Have you had a promotion or raise in the last year?	____	
5.	Have you had a promotion or raise for at least two successive years?	____	
6.	Is your salary equal to or greater than your age?	____	
7.	Have your performance reviews at work been positive?	____	
8.	As you measure your career progress through promotions and raises are you keeping up with or surpassing the "norm" established for your career?	____	
9.	Do you know what responsibilities/accomplishments you need to master in order to make it to the next level?	____	
10.	Do you enjoy, and are you challenged by your job?	____	
11.	Are you satisfied with your career progress to date?	____	

Part II. Your Physical Side

The raw material of your image. Check yourself out in a mirror, without makeup or special grooming.

		Yes	No
12.	Is your overall body fit and firm?	____	
13.	Does your body's fitness give you the energy to go through the workday with ease?	____	
14.	Without makeup, is your skin clear of bumps, broken capillaries, and brown spots?	____	
15.	Are you doing all you can to keep your skin youthful and firm?	____	
16.	Does your hair still have a youthful shine and color?	____	

Extra
Edge

		Yes	No

17. Do you have a hairstyle that is attractive and easily managed?   _____   ▦

18. Does your posture reflect confidence?   _____   ▦

Part III. Your Physical Image on the Job

19. Have you stopped wearing the same style outfits you had when you first started working?   _____   ▦

20. Have you changed your professional image to match your professional position?   _____   ▦

21. Have you realized the importance of individuality to your career image?   _____   ▦

22. Are you satisfied with the way you wear your clothes at work?   _____   ▦

23. Have you realized the drawbacks of the "uniform" approach to professional dress?   _____   ▦

24. Have you learned how to use makeup to achieve an attractive look that suits a professional woman?   _____   ▦

25. Do you use makeup to make the most of your looks?   _____   ▦

26. Does your on-the-job appearance convey a sense of individuality, sophistication, and style?   _____   ▦

27. Have you updated your makeup and hairstyle to reflect your growing career sophistication?   _____   ▦

28. Have you been able to incorporate sophisticated femininity into your professional image?   _____   ▦

29. Have you learned to camouflage your less-than-perfect physical aspects?   _____   ▦

30. Do you know how to use accessories to enhance your professional image?   _____   ▦

Image
Quotient

The IQ Test (Continued)

Part IV. Your Non-Physical Career Image

	Yes	No
31. Are you respected at work by your superiors?	___	▨
32. Are you respected by your peers and subordinates?	___	▨
33. Do people view you as someone with strong potential at your company?	___	▨
34. Can you get attention and hold the floor at meetings without difficulty?	___	▨
35. Are you confident when you have to make an oral presentation?	___	▨
36. Have you learned how to create positive visibility on the job through your day-to-day interactions?	___	▨
37. Do you exude energy and vitality throughout the business day?	___	▨
38. Do you understand office politics and use it to your advantage?	___	▨
39. Do your voice and manner display a sense of authority and a confidence in your ability to get the job done?	___	▨
40. Do you enjoy interviews, looking upon them as a positive opportunity to move up in your career?	___	▨

Scoring and Analysis

While there are no correct or incorrect answers to the previous questions, the way that you answer is an indication of how well you are doing in your career and how successful your professional image is. The white boxes are an indication of a career that is moving along well, enhanced by a mature, competent, and professional image. If you are serious about advancing in the corporate world, you should be striving to have as many of your answers as possible fall into the white boxes.

Now that you are thinking about your professional image and how it plays an integral role in your career, read on! The remainder of the book will focus on strategies for creating a total professional style.

Extra
Edge

Part II

Developing Your Own Total Professional Style

Chapter 7

Power Dressing,

Part I: Update on Dressing for Success

From our interviews with successful women Harvard Business School graduates we learned that as a woman progresses in her career she becomes more confident, more self-assured, and more interested in expressing her own individuality. Early in their careers, many of these women became stifled by their inability to express their uniqueness through traditional "uniform" dress. The uniform made them feel no different from their peers. While this may sound wonderfully egalitarian—all of us being equal—it's not a winning attitude for the woman who wants to be a success.

Are You Special?

HARVARD STUDY QUESTION

Do you feel that the clothes you wear on the job are one way of expressing your individuality while still maintaining your professionalism?

Sixty-three percent of the women interviewed felt that the way they dressed was an important aspect of maintaining their sense of individuality within the organization. These Harvard women know that to get to the top, you have to feel that you are individual and special—that there's something that sets you apart from the other people in the organization. After all, only a small percentage of business people ever make it to the top. And a sure part of success comes from your inner psychology. But if every time you look in the mirror you see a replica of 100 other women in your organization, you can't help but start to feel that you don't have anything special to offer, that you are just like everyone else. And that can lead to big problems in your career.

Now I'm not going to stand on a soapbox and spend the next chapter discussing the psychological implications of the inner consciousness. But I do want to get one point across. Your style of executive dress and image can go a long way toward making you feel that you not only belong in the organization—but more importantly—that you are uniquely special to that organization.

Power Dressing for the New Executive Woman

Today's smart executive woman doesn't want to be packaged into a uniform—she wants to convey her power and authority while at the same time expressing her individuality and her attractiveness. A few years ago that was a difficult task. The executive woman was faced with either being straight-jacketed into a drab business uniform, or wearing an outfit that was considered better on the cocktail circuit.

Times have indeed changed. You can now select from a variety of dresses, suits, and outfits that are well-made, attractive, and yet totally professional. The only problem confronting you now is a lack of time to peruse the countless stores in search of appropriate outfits.

Although a number of forward-looking stores have set up special departments with well-versed consultants to advise the executive woman with her wardrobe needs, most stores do not provide this service. This chapter is meant to guide you in your selection process.

Before I begin, there are two new trends in retailing of which you should be aware. The first is that many stores are providing "personal shoppers" or "image consultants" for your assistance. These consultants will help to develop an entire wardrobe or merely pick out one item to complete an outfit. And they are usually very good at creating a well-dressed look. But unless these women have specific training in "executive dressing," you can't be sure that you are getting the best advice on clothes for the office. Remember, executive dressing is a very specific form of dressing well. An outfit that is perfectly appropriate for non-business functions may not work at all in the office.

The other development in retailing that can spell problems for professional women is the new and lucrative business of "dressing the corporate woman." While I am all for new styles and clothes, as you will see in this chapter, I am concerned that many designers are marketing or promoting lines under an "executive look" label that are completely inappropriate for the office. Recently, I inspected a new line that was supposedly developed for professional women, and I can tell you right now that you're not going to be viewed as an authoritative executive in those clothes!

The clothes discussed in this chapter have been chosen to convey, first and foremost, the image of authority, and then style, attractiveness, and individuality. Your clothes must all be well-made and timeless. In other words, your wardrobe should be essentially wearable five years from now with only minor accessory changes. The emphasis should be on classic lines, colors, and materials.

Dressing for Authority

There are a few general guidelines that you should always follow when considering an outfit or an article of clothing for your professional wardrobe:

- Dark, rich colors generally convey more class and "power," than light, bright colors.

- Wear subdued prints and stripes rather than large, floral designs.

- Simple lines and styles are more appropriate for the office than fussy or very detailed clothes.

- Always wear quality fabrics—natural fibers instead of man-made.

- Always wear well-made clothes—hems that are even and unnoticeable; lapels that lie flat; seams that don't pucker.

- Select shoes, handbags, briefcases and watches on the basis of quality materials and sleek, classic lines.

- Use accessories to "complete" your look—wear belts, earrings, necklaces.

- Avoid trendy styles at the office, such as puffed sleeves and exaggerated shoulders, as they are generally inappropriate.

Leave The Uniform to The Army

You will not find the "uniform" here—that prefabricated suit with a minimum of style and a complete absence of individuality. I hope I have convinced you by now that to the extent that you suppress your individuality by adopting a cookie-cutter uniform, you decrease your chances of career success.

So let's move onward and upward. Let's get out of the uniform and into clothes that are just as authoritative and professional looking—but which show that we are confident enough to add a touch of panache. The following styles represent the look of the '80's for the executive woman.

DRESS...(ING) for Success

Contrary to what you may have been told about the necessity of suits for businesswomen, you can create a completely professional look with a dress. Designers today have created dresses that are authoritative, stylish, comfortable, and completely appropriate for the office. You no longer have to select between a fancy cocktail dress or a fluffy flowered concoction. Many of today's styles can enhance your image as well as a suit can.

In dresses, as in suits, the most important elements in addition to craftsmanship are color, fabric, and design. While some consultants recommend flower prints and pastels, I would consider these dresses carefully before I bought one for the office. It has been my experience that, in general, it's difficult for a woman to convey a strong professional image when she's wearing a powder blue or soft pink dress. These colors usually conjure up images of sweetness and innocence. It can be done, but it takes a very self-assured woman in a very powerful position to carry it off.

The dresses illustrated convey this new attitude toward executive dressing. Notice their somewhat architectural design—strong, clean lines that tend to make the wearer appear tall and slim. There are no constricting styles, no fluffy flounces, no delicate, "impossible-to-work-in" details. These are working clothes that let you get down to business.

Extra
Edge

Dress...ing for Success

Do add dresses to your business wardrobe. Today's executive woman feels as confident in the right dress as she does in a suit.

Extra
Edge

Select dresses that convey an authoritative and confident image—look for clean lines and few details. When you want to add a bit more formality to your dress, add a jacket.

You will notice that there are no short sleeves or sleeveless dresses, which are inappropriate for most executive offices. If you wish to wear a short-sleeved dress, you should wear a jacket with it and keep it on.

As with all the other clothing items, I recommend dresses made from natural fibers. I've found the best materials for dresses—those that give a professional look while still being comfortable—are wool, wool challis, wool flannel, and silk or combinations of these materials. In the summertime, silk, challis, cotton, and linen (especially the non-wrinkle type) will maintain your executive image.

Colors that work well in dresses are again the deep rich colors such as navy, black, burgundy, red, charcoal grey, teal, brown, rust, steel or royal blue, and slate, and lighter colors such as grey, beige or dusty rose. Stripes, checks, prints, and other designs are best in deep colors or combined with white. I don't recommend light bright colors such as turquoise, orange, or lime.

Tan, light grey, beige, cream, or white are good colors for the summer months, as are certain dark colors, such as black and navy. Soft colors can work well in the summer; if you want to wear them try to balance their "softness" by making sure that the dress has strong lines. If you wear a soft color in a soft style you may come across as too young or unprofessional. Look for "iced" colors, which are generally white with a subtle hint of another color—iced mint, for example, has a slight touch of mint green.

Most of the dresses shown have a strong collar or high neckline. This is important for several reasons. First, and obviously, too low a neckline is inappropriate for the office, and always will be. Second, with a high neckline, you have the option of wearing a blazer over the dress to create a suit-like appearance. Thus, if you enjoy the ease and comfort of a dress but still prefer to effect the look of a suit for special times during the day, you can simply add the blazer.

Two-Piece Dresses

A matching skirt and blouse, which give the appearance of a dress when worn together, also works well for the office. These two-piece dresses provide a number of different looks. The skirt and blouse can be worn together, or coordinated with your other clothes to create additional outfits. See the versatility in the two piece combinations illustrated.

Not only do you have the flexibility afforded by mixing and matching the pieces, but when they are worn together and topped by a blazer, you can create another

Two-Piece Dressing—Mix or Match

Two piece dressing (matching skirt and blouse) adds versatility to your wardrobe.
Wear the two pieces together, add a belt and you have a "dress."
Or create a number of new looks by mixing the individual pieces with other skirts and blouses.
When you wear the pieces separately, always add a jacket.
An unmatched skirt and blouse is usually too informal for most offices.

Extra
Edge

professional looking outfit. Look for graphic prints, paisleys, stripes, or solid color dresses with tiny designs.

If you like the look of a blazer over a dress or two-piece outfit, you can create a more interesting and attractive look by using a solid blazer over a striped or print design. For best results, match the color of your blazer to a color in the dress or outfit.

Coordinate Chic

A number of professional looking outfits can be created with coordinates—jackets and skirts that blend together rather than match. This does not mean, however, that you can throw together a jacket and a skirt without taking the time to tie them together. It helps if your outfit has a theme; for example, if your jacket is solid black, select a skirt that has black in the design. Or create a monochromatic look with your skirt and blouse, e.g., a charcoal grey skirt and ice grey blouse with your black jacket.

You can also use brighter colors when you wear coordinates. While a red suit may be too flashy or overpowering, a red skirt balanced by a more subdued jacket and blouse will appear professional. With coordinates you can create a number of elegant, professional and individualistic outfits by mixing colors, lines, and fabrics. Try a cashmere jacket with a silk surah paisley skirt. Add a cream colored silk blouse. For more ideas of styles that work well together, see the coordinates illustration.

Suited for Success

Suits will always be with us—for good reason. They are classic, versatile, and professional. The new emphasis on clothes for working women has meant greater attention to making business suits stylish and attractive. In fact, a number of designers who formerly created suits for men are now designing suits for women.

These new suits are not men's suits sized for women—rather they are a synthesis of styles specifically designed for women with the custom tailoring and excellent fabrics that are staples of a quality man's suit. The difference between these suits and the original business suits for women is as vast as that between the Model T and today's Mercedes.

Coordinating Your Looks—Coordinate Chic

Coordinates are a great alternative to the suit.
They are completely professional and yet give greater freedom and variety to your outfits.
Show your personal style in your choice of coordinates.

Extra
Edge

Suited for Success

The new look in business suits—softer construction, more assured, more style without compromising your professional appearance.

Shown are examples of contemporary suits for women that work well in the executive suite. The illustrations should give you an idea of the range of suits that are appropriate for business · You should avoid large pattern and prints because, as always, subtlety has style.

Suits are generally more authoritative and elegant if they are in dark, or rich colors such as navy, black, burgundy, teal, brown, charcoal grey, steel blue or deep rust. But this does not mean that your suits have to appear drab, nor does it mean that you have to wear solid colors. Tweeds, pinstripes, herringbones, small-patterned plaids and checks are fine.

Light colors can also work well in the office, especially in the warmer months, although you have to take special care to ensure that they do not appear too soft or too sweet-looking. Colors such as white, tan, dusty rose, and light grey are good professional colors for warm climates or temperatures. I do think it is more difficult for a woman to have professional impact when she wears pastel-colored suits and dresses, but even then, the right style and fabric can determine the professionalism of the look. When you wear bright colors make sure that the lines are clean and uncluttered and the fabric is top quality.

Summertime or warmer climates can present problems in maintaining a professional image. In hot weather, many women become less particular about the clothes they wear. This is a mistake. Designers often use very bright, splashy colors like purple or fuchsia for their summer clothes. You should think twice before adding these to your business wardrobe, particularly if you're in a conservative industry such as banking or law. Many of these colors are really for cruise or casual wear.

Safari suits or the short sleeved/sleeveless outfits that tend to crop up during the warmer months convey little authority and are simply too informal for the office. They have the same low-image impact as a businessman wearing a leisure suit or a short sleeved shirt.

Some of the most professional and impressive fabrics are wool, wool flannel, wool crepe, gabardine, mohair, cashmere, raw silk, cotton velvet, cotton, and linen. These fabrics breathe, maintain their shape, are expensive-looking (and expensive), and wear well. Some of the materials are best for jackets; others work well for both jackets and skirts. Gabardines and lightweight wools can be worn at least nine months out of the year, and possibly more.

In addition to the materials listed above, wool challis, silk surah, and silk are excellent materials for skirts. I don't recommend man-made fabrics except in extremely unusual circumstances. Despite claims that there have been major improvements in artificial fibers, I still don't feel that you can beat the look of the natural fibers.

Blouses

Even if you work in the most conservative industries, you can add a spark of individuality to your outfit with the right blouse. You can also soften an otherwise austere look by selecting a blouse with just a hint of femininity. I am not recommending blouses with lavish frills or ruffles—they are out of place in most companies. I am suggesting blouses that have subtle details of craftsmanship.

Break out of the mold. Throw away the skinny ribbon at the neck that is part of the "uniform." Instead of wearing a man-tailored blouse, even if it's silk, look for some of the styles suggested below. Try a mandarin collar, a roll collar, a V-neck, or a round neckline to create your own personal look. What about a white crepe blouse with a pleated front as illustrated?

Extra Edge

Blouses

You don't have to wear the standard man-tailored blouse anymore.
Blouses today have a style and an elegance that are perfect for the office.
Soften your suit with a more feminine, but never frilly, blouse.

Almost any color blouse will be suitable as long as it isn't so vivid that you receive comments about it. Always buy quality blouses in fabrics such as silk, linen, challis, and crepe. Don't wear blouses so sheer that you can see your bra or slip. Even if you have a jacket over it, people will notice.

Pants Problems

Despite the fact that they provide the most comfort and actually are the most practical approach to clothing, pants in general are still frowned upon in business, with a few exceptions. In certain industries, such as sales, production, and engineering, they may be acceptable. But if no one in your company wears them, don't be a trendsetter.

If you opt for pants in your position, be meticulous about the fit. If you don't have a flawless pants figure, don't wear them! Keep the style simple, or try a trouser style—but make sure the legs are straight, neither flared nor tapered. Wear only dark rich colors (light colors only in warmer months) and buy natural fabrics such as wool. Never wear polyester pants!

Corporate Cloak

Your coat is also important to your professional image, even if you think people only see it for a few minutes before you hang it in the closet at work. Some women wear any old coat to work and think that no one will notice. They're wrong. Besides, what happens when you have to leave the office to meet with important clients? The first thing they will see is your coat.

For the most part, there are really only a few basic styles that are good for the executive woman. I recommend strong, uncluttered lines and solid colors. Wool works well, but if you want to consider your coat as an investment, opt for a nicer luxury fabric such as cashmere, mohair, or camel's hair. I have a camel's hair coat that gives the appearance of cashmere but wears like iron.

Avoid coats that are very fitted (too difficult to wear a suit underneath) or have trendy detailing—wide lapels, big shoulders, rolled cuffs. Stay away from big plaids or colors that don't mix well with other colors. You want a coat to look luxurious, wear well, and stay in style for a long time. The styles illustrated are samples of classic coats that "go to work," and then look good when you're out on the town.

Starter Wardrobe

If you're just starting out in business, a good beginning wardrobe would consist of:

1. Two dark solid-color suits

2. Several light-color, good-quality silk blouses in different styles

3. A basic, dark dress

4. A two-piece dress

5. A classic coat

6. Some variety of accessories

7. Several skirts of different styles: pleated, A line, dirndl

Corporate Cloaks

Look for coats with clean lines and strong but luxurious-looking fabrics
such as camel hair, mohair, cashmere, or wool.
You want your coat to look stylish whether you're wearing it to work or at night.
Make sure that your coat allows enough room for you to wear a suit underneath.

With each items of clothing that you buy, look for a color that will work well with most of the other clothes in your wardrobe.

Now is *not* the time to buy "memorable" clothes—a dress or a suit that really stands out. You are going to be wearing these clothes a lot, and you only want people to remember that you are always well-dressed—not to remember that you are always wearing the same dress or suit.

Since you will be wearing a jacket most of the time, either as part of a suit or over your dresses, buy a dark, solid color suit or jacket. Don't feel that you need a two-button fitted blazer. Look for some of the more versatile classic styles as shown at the beginning of this chapter. Not only will they look more sophisticated than the traditional blazer, but they will work better with the variety of skirt styles for today's professional woman.

Keep most of the pieces in your initial wardrobe dark and solid. Use the two-piece dress and the blouses to add brightness and color to your outfits. Look for subtle prints or stripes for the two-piece dress—these can then mix and match with the solid suit jackets and skirts to give a good variety to your daily "look."

For the one-piece dress, I recommend a dark rich color, a versatile material and a classic style. Then use your accessories to change the overall look of the dress—dress it up one day with bright eye-catching accessories, or emphasize its strong lines and styling by wearing just a few small accessories. A silk dress will be versatile enough to take you from the office to an elegant club with a few minor accessory changes. Look for a dress that has a stand up collar during the day and is opened at night for a "sexier" look.

As you add a few pieces to your basic wardrobe, make sure that they will work with the rest of your wardrobe. If they don't, but something else. Wait until you are ahead in your finances before buying clothes that will stand out or only complement one or two pieces in your wardrobe. Never sacrifice quality to buy more clothes—your image is critical to your success, whether it is your first day on the job or your tenth year.

Since you will probably be wearing your coat everyday during the cold months, I recommend buying a coat in a neutral color so that it will complement your outfits. If you look for classic styling—no fitted waist or small shoulders—then you should be able to wear it over your jackets.

When your wardrobe is in its development phase, you will have to rely heavily on accessories to create new looks for the same suit. I discuss accessories in depth in the next chapter, where you will see how to create a variety of different looks by changing accessories.

Image Makers—Image Breakers

The following is a list of suggestions to keep in mind when you're dressing for Total Professional Style:

- Double or triple check the fit of your suit or dress—make sure that the shoulders fit properly, the fabric doesn't pull across the bust or the derriere, and the underarms are not too tight.

- Opt for quality rather than quantity—don't buy inexpensive items because you feel you must increase your wardrobe.

- Keep skirt length at knee level or not longer than mid-calf. And never wear skirts above your knees.

- Avoid soft fluffy angora-type sweaters—they're much too feminine and soft-looking.

- Don't substitute faddy items for classic clothing—culottes for skirts, faddy pants, sailor blouses.

- Never wear anything too tight, too low-cut, too bright, too clingy, too anything.

- Be very careful when dressing in pastels—they have a tendency to soften your image.

- Glittery/metallic clothing is meant for nighttime only—not the office.

- Leave tiered skirts for fun or casual wear.

- Avoid anything preppie—monogrammed sweaters, Fair Isle sweaters, bright print skirts. That's fine for a non-office look, but inappropriate in a corporation.

Chapter 8

Power Dressing
Part II: Authority Accessories

Accessories, more than ever before, are playing a major role in completing and defining a professional image. They give versatility to your wardrobe, and add important elements of individuality and femininity.

Formulating Your Total Look

Accessories are everything in pulling your look together. They provide important elements of class and style to your image. The right accessories can both enhance a polished image and help you create a number of different office looks with the same basic wardrobe.

In this chapter we talk about the use of accessories for the office: when and how quality counts, how to change your outfit with them, and which accessories are appropriate for the office and which are not. In *Chapter 18, Business By Day, Glamour By Night,* we also discuss the use of accessories and their role in changing a day look (or an office look) into a night (or a glamourous) look.

Extra
Edge

Executive Earrings

There is a new look in earrings today and it goes well with the dress styles we have been discussing. The line in both clothes and earrings is strong and unfussy. It's a perfect look for the executive woman.

Generally speaking, in the very conservative industries such as banking and law, the smaller the earring the better. This does not mean that you are confined to tiny stud earrings. Earrings that are roughly the size of a nickel are acceptable in even the most conservative companies. Stud earrings are always appropriate, whatever your industry, but if you're in the less conservative areas you should consider the new styles. I do not recommend the dangling earrings that resemble tiny chandeliers, or earrings that move noticeably when you move your head. While they may be fine for social occasions, they are too distracting and frivolous for most businesses.

Some of the styles that are appropriate for the office are illustrated just to show you the variety of shapes and designs that you can use to spice up your office wardrobe. As you'll note, many of the shapes seem to come from your old geometry books!

Executive
Earrings
A Variety of Shapes.

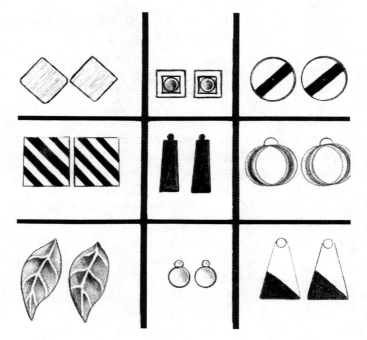

Expensive materials or metals such as gold, silver, platinum, bronze, pewter, onyx, and lapis are always suitable for the office. (Quality is never inappropriate!). I would be careful with diamonds—small studs may be suitable but the larger, showier ones should be reserved for evening wear. Pearl studs are always appropriate for the office.

Today's "costume" jewelry is not only acceptable for the office but in many cases is more appropriate than "real" jewelry. But even in costume jewelry, you should look for quality and taste. As an example, in the illustration of the earrings, those shown could be gold-filled, or done in pewter, or composed of man-made materials such as plastic or ceramic.

Colored earrings are best in the same strong colors we have mentioned for your clothes, such as black, burgundy, navy, or white. There are two things you should remember if you buy "gold-toned" or "gold-colored" jewelry: to make sure the "gold" color resembles the real thing (those that are obviously fake have a dreadful yellow cast), and to stop wearing the item when the gold color begins to disintegrate (which it will, often too quickly).

Necklaces

While strands of pearls and gold chains remain standard necklaces for professional women, there are many acceptable alternatives to these traditional accessories. Strands of beads made of garnet, lapis, and onyx are distinctive yet still professional. Buy a long strand of these beads and tie a knot near the end for an eye-catching necklace. Then you will have two "different" accessory looks from one piece—wear the strand the standard way or "knot" it for a new look. I have also found that certain types of choker necklaces and pins (not cameos) add "dash" to blouses with stand-up collars.

There are also new types of necklace designs that are appropriate for the office and add a spark of individuality to your executive dress. As with earrings and other accessories, the more conservative the industry, the smaller the jewelry should be. But many of the new necklaces, such as those below, are appropriate for most industries. Some of the designers call these pieces sculpture instead of jewelry. And indeed, they can be works of art.

Bracelets

There are some bracelets that are appropriate for the office. Look for those that can be worn alone such as a metal wrist band. The best type of bracelet is one that adds a finishing touch to your outfit, but is somewhat stationary and quiet. The

Stepping Out

Shoes are an important part of your professional appearance.
And styles have never been better.

main problem with many bracelets is that they are meant to be worn in clusters of three, four, even more. They slide up and down your forearm, hitting and clicking against each other and, in general, making office life difficult. Charm bracelets, regardless of their sentimental value, are not professional. Nor are any bracelets or bangles which make writing difficult.

Belts

You should consider a belt as vital a component of your suit (and your dress) as a man does. Even if your suit has a waistband that doesn't require a belt, you should add one anyway. It completes your look. The best belts are leather, in the dark rich colors we have discussed. I have always found the look of a textured belt such as snakeskin or lizard to be especially attractive and rich-looking.

In the very conservative industries the belt should generally be one-half to three-fourths of an inch wide when used with a suit. In the less conservative industries such as advertising, marketing, media, and retailing, wider belts and sashes are also suitable. Many dresses, such as the styles which we have discussed previously, also work well with both thin and wide belts. A different belt can change the look of a dress substantially. The width generally should be between three-fourths of an inch and two inches.

Sashes, such as a striped silk, can add panache to an otherwise severe suit without disrupting an executive appearance. Look for interesting buckles to add dash to your outfit. Again, keep in mind the rule that the more conservative the industry, the smaller the accessory.

Shoe Signals

The shoe industry has come on strong in the last few years with a variety of interesting and appropriate designs for the office. The basic pump is no longer basic. It is available in a variety of colors and styles with different heel shapes and sizes.

The classic pump is usually the most flattering to your leg—it elongates it and makes you appear taller and slimmer. Straps have a tendency to look "little-girlish" and to break up the line of your leg. Slingback styles are also suitable for most offices and many women find them extremely comfortable. A slight toe-opening, particularly in the warmer months, can be both professional and comfortable.

In the conservative industries you are generally safer (if that's what you want) with colors such as grey, black, brown, taupe, navy, and beige. These colors are obviously fine for all industries, but if you want a little less conservatism, you can wear other colors: such as wine, loden, red, yellow, or melon. Spectators, in navy, brown, or black with white, are semi-conservative classics for warm weather wear.

Although you have an attractive array of styles and colors from which to choose, you do not have a choice in the material. Your shoes should *always* be leather—I recommend looking for shoes with both leather uppers and lowers. This shouldn't really limit your selection—you can wear lizard, snakeskin, or woven leather shoes if you want a different look. Avoid inexpensive shoes, as they are very easy to spot and can destroy an otherwise professional appearance.

"Can I Walk In Them?"

The most important question you should ask yourself when buying a pair of shoes for work is "Can I walk in them?" It's ridiculous, of course, but many women who should know better buy shoes that confine them to walking three feet an hour. You never know when you will be with a group of business associates and have to walk five or six blocks or when you have to run for an elevator or a taxi. It won't do a thing for your image (especially if the rest of them are men), if they have to keep stopping so that you can catch up. Leave the delicate sandals and super-high heels for non-business times.

Extra
Edge

Speaking of heels, you should wear neither flats nor spike heels to work. A good executive should have a heel that is between one inch and three inches in height. No more, no less.

One last thing about your shoes. Always make sure they are polished or shined. Scuff marks are not part of the executive image (even if you have been climbing up the corporate ladder!).

Stockings

A well-known male consultant has advised women to wear only one type of stocking—a standard, clear, tan shade. On the contrary, a wide variety of stockings can be worn in business and, are considered appropriate for the office.

When choosing sheer stockings, the best colors for a conservative look are natural, grey, taupe, soft brown, navy, or black. In warm weather months, some of the cream or pastel colors work well with light-colored outfits. Opaque stockings in colors such as black, dark brown, charcoal, and navy are also acceptable in a cold climate business setting.

Textured stockings can now be seen in the executive suite. As long as their texture and the design are subtle, the stockings will complete your office look perfectly. Leave the new lace or polka-dotted stockings and any glittery designs for non-business times.

If you are in the less conservative industries, you can also try a splash of color such as wine, blueberry, or loden in stockings to accent the stripes or print of your outfit.

Handbags for the Professional

The key word in handbags, as in shoes, is leather. Invest in a good leather handbag in black, burgundy, or dark brown—your best bet is to match the color of the shoes that you wear the most. A handbag with a permanent shoulder strap or a clutch that can turn into a shoulder bag is the most practical for the business woman. Since you will usually have your briefcase with you, a shoulder bag will be easier to carry. If you want a handbag to work in warm and cold months, look for a neutral color such as taupe.

A clutch can also be placed in your briefcase to decrease the number of items you have to carry. Many women find that a small clutch that holds their cards, cash, and makeup can easily be carried in their briefcase.

A word about designer handbags, briefcases, wallets, glass cases, and similar accessories. If you like them because of the styling and the leather quality, buy them. But don't buy the ones with designer initials covering every centimeter. (Besides, one of the most famous lines is only vinyl, anyway). They no longer add to your image. And while everyone knows that they are expensive, everybody seems to have them now—real or fake.

Some of the famous designers do, however, make excellent quality leather goods without their initials. And you really can't surpass the craftsmanship or the leather quality. So, if you prefer designer products, look for the non-initialed styles.

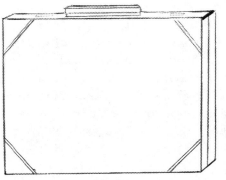

Executive Briefcases
Invest in a good one

Briefcases

As in the case of most accessories, quality counts. You should only use a leather briefcase. In my opinion, the darker the leather, such as black, dark brown, or burgundy, the more expensive the look. When you are investing in a briefcase, (and you should consider it an investment), look for those with sleek lines. They have much more style than the wide, boxy types. You might also consider the soft, unstructured briefcases. They work much better with the new suits and dresses.

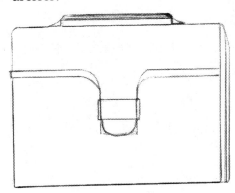

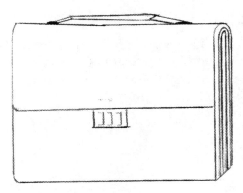

Extra
Edge

Power Watches

A good watch for a professional woman is one that is expensive (no getting around that), classic, and strong. By expensive, I mean in the area of $150 to $400. Beware of ostentatiously expensive watches, which can actually have a negative image impact. A good classic watch should denote time in the standard manner—with hands—not with flashing lights, music, or digitals. And a strong watch should have clean lines, a good-sized face, and a solid strap or metal band.

To put it another way, I would recommend avoiding those watches that are clearly for women—with tiny faces, decorative flourishes, and skinny bands. And while it should go without saying, I'll say it anyway—never wear a gimmicky watch such as those with a caricature or cartoon face.

If you prefer a watch with a strap, it should be of lizard, snakeskin, or a similar leather. And it should be in a deep color such as black—straps in tan or pastels are not as rich-looking. If you prefer a metal band, you should buy only gold-filled (if you can't afford all gold) or silver-filled. If only the finish is gold or silver, it will wear off rather quickly and you will be left with a very cheap-looking watch. That's why it pays in the long run to buy gold-filled.

Jewelry to Avoid

Certain kinds of jewelry can be image destroying. These pieces may be attractive and appropriate under non-business circumstances but they are not right for the office:

- Loose-fitting bracelets, especially jingling, noisy ones such as charm bracelets, or a cluster of hoop bracelets tracking up your arm.

- Fancy rings—or rings on several fingers. One or two subtle rings are all you should wear to the office.

- Bead or chain necklaces in clusters of four or more.

I'm sure you see the point. Anything that is noisy, appears frivolous, or can tangle should be eliminated from your office wardrobe. There is nothing sillier than a professional woman trying to untangle bracelets caught in her necklaces during a business meeting!

Chapter 9

Corporate Camouflage—
"All's Fair in Love and War" ... and Business!

Now let's look at some of the physical career liabilities that we've discussed in previous chapters and how to "hide" them. After all, everything is fair when the objective is survival on the corporate battlefield!

It's important that you understand when I call something a liability, I am not making a judgment of good or bad. As used here, a liability is an image element that for any number of reasons generates a negative impression in business. In fact, some of these "liabilities" are considered assets outside of the corporate world.

Are You Being "Overlooked" Because You're Short?

Being short can be an asset, but I have never seen it help in the business world. A short woman can seem "cute," "helpless," and little girlish, all of which can be damaging to her career. Being short diminishes your sense of authority and power, and often, people, (particularly men), feel protective of a small woman. But this can lead to problems in business. In many instances, the less threatened a man is, the less respect he gives.

Being short does not have to be a negative factor. Many famous and powerful women are much smaller than the public would ever imagine. A combination of the right attitude and the right image have helped them to convey a sense of strength and power. Madame Rubenstein was tiny (4"10'), yet few dared to oppose her when she ruthlessly built her cosmetics empire. Who ever thinks of Nancy Reagan at 5"1' as weak?

The first step in dealing with shortness is to look within yourself. Do you act small? Do you play helpless and little girlish? Are you like Debbie Reynolds, perennially cute? If so, start thinking of yourself as a mature businesswoman, one who is self-reliant and strong. Try standing tall. (All the books tell you this, and that's because it really does work. Standing tall stretches the spine to its maximum height and you can actually gain a couple of inches). Perhaps you should consider taking ballet lessons—ballet is great for developing a strong erect posture. Eliminate any cute mannerisms you may have cultivated. Think and act as if you are a strong, tall businesswoman, and others will begin to think of you that way. And then turn to *Tips on Creating a Tall Appearance* in this chapter for further help.

Tips on Creating a Tall Appearance

There are a number of practical and easy ways to create the physical illusion of being taller than you are:

- Eliminate from your business wardrobe such frilly or little girl touches as Peter Pan collars, ruffles, sailor dresses, cap sleeves. If you like the look, save it for non-business occasions.

- Avoid innocent or pastel colors and prints. Skip preppie accessories like headbands, barrettes, or shoes with a flower at the toe.

- You can create a longer, slimmer look by keeping tops and bottoms in the same color family. This gives the illusion of one long, unbroken line.

- To appear taller, you want the eye to move from your toes to your face in one long sweep, which also means that most of your accessories and color interest should be near your face. Use scarves, necklaces, and earrings to keep focus on this area.

- When you wear dresses, look for strong, solid colors and accentuate them with interesting necklaces and earrings. You will look taller than you would in light print dresses with contrasting belts.

- Keep belts in the same color as your dress or skirt rather than bisecting your body visually with a contrasting belt—which makes you appear shorter.

- Stay away from dresses or skirts with contrasting colors or patterns at the hemline. If you like stripes, make sure that you select vertical ones.

- A suit with a straight-falling, long, lean jacket and an equally dark skirt will also give the illusion of height. Wear a bright or light blouse with it to focus attention on your upper body.

- If you wear coordinated pieces, wear the lighter or brighter color in the jacket. Or wear an impact color (such as red) near your face, in the jacket, blouse, or as a floppy bow at the neck.

- If you prefer styles that usually look better on taller women, such as capes, scale the style to your size. When you experiment with some of the newer fashions always stand away from a full-length mirror and look for the long, lean line. If the style doesn't give it, leave it alone.

- Dark stockings and shoes worn with dark outfits also increase the impression of height. As do light stocking and shoes worn with light outfits. The key is continuation of color. If you continue the color of your dress into your shoes and stockings, your body line appears longer. Contrasting shoes and stockings "cut" your body line.

- Pumps create a longer look to your legs. Shoes with straps tend to make your legs appear shorter than pumps cut low to the toe.

- Look for a hairstyle that doesn't overpower you with its length or make you appear pixie-ish if it's too short. If you like longish hair, look for the new haircuts that give the illusion of length without making you look top heavy.

Extra
Edge

- Wear makeup to give you a sophisticated look. The short woman has the problem (problem?!) of sometimes looking younger than she really is. You don't want to look too young or inexperienced for the job. Stay away from the young, innocent-looking makeup colors like soft pinks and blues. They'll only add to a little-girl look.

When Being Well-Endowed is a Bust

We've already discussed the research that indicates that big-busted women are perceived as being less intelligent and less competent than smaller busted women. Of course it isn't true, but do you really want to spend your day trying to convince people that their impression of you is totally off the mark? Wouldn't you rather devote your time to more career-oriented projects?

Obviously no executive woman wants to be considered either less intelligent or less competent than her peers. And the worst mistake you can make is to try to hide your bust by hunching your shoulders. It only makes you look meek and timid. Many women with large busts unconsciously adopt this posture after years of attracting unwanted stares and remarks about their figure. (Besides, it doesn't work anyway).

So instead of tilting at windmills, if you are large-busted, look for clothes that will divert attention from your bust and direct it to your total appearance. There are a number of ways to do so, as I show in *Tips for Minimizing Your Bust*. You will feel more confident and you will carry yourself in a more positive manner as a result.

Tips for Minimizing Your Bust

- Avoid dresses that are fitted, figure-hugging, or emphasize your figure in any way.

- Be careful with soft clingy materials which will emphasize the lines of your figure.

- The brighter the dress, the more attention it will receive and so will your figure.

- Deep, dark colors will tend to disguise your figure more than light, bright colors.

Corporate
Camouflage

- Be discriminating about dresses with pinched waists—more often than not they will exaggerate your bustline. Look for loose-fitting tops and silky fabrics that don't add bulk or have stiff lines.

- Suits are your best bet. The right jacket can successfully disguise an ample bust. Look for loose, somewhat unstructured jackets that don't hug the body or nip in at the waist.

- Look for narrow lapels or no lapels, since wide or fancy lapels draw attention to the jacket and hence your bustline. Make sure that the jacket hangs smoothly, and does not "gap" around the bustline.

- It is also best for you to stick with straight uncluttered lines in your skirts. Puffy skirts or dirndls will only exaggerate your hourglass tendencies.

- Always make sure that your blouse doesn't gap in front. Nothing can detract more from an otherwise professional image. If your blouses have a tendency to do this, consider having them specially made, or at least fitted by a seamstress.

- The right bra will also provide good support, and will help minimize your bustline. You don't want to be known as the woman with the jiggle—leave that for the television starlets! Look for bras that are bust minimizers or have soft shapes rather than the old-fashioned stiff ones.

Are You Getting a Little Too Big for The Job?

If you're like most people, you'll tend to agree with the old saying that "you can't be too thin." And if you're like most, you think you could be thinner. Obviously there is only one way to be thinner—exercise and eat less—but there are ways to look thinner while you're getting there.

The clothes you choose can make a critical difference in your appearance. Choose the wrong styles or the wrong colors and you can look as if you lost the battle of the bulge. With a careful eye, you can create the illusion of a slimmer figure. And the best news of all is that designers are now paying attention to the woman who weighs more than 90 pounds, dripping wet.

Extra
Edge

Follow the general rule in all your dressing: play down the parts of your figure that you don't want to be noticed, and play up those aspects that add positively to your appearance. Remember, dark colors "play down;" light colors draw attention. Fitted garments accentuate; loose lines hide.

Look for the styles that have slimming potential. Don't try to hide your body under a formless tent dress. Not only doesn't it hide your weight, it adds to the overall impression of out-of-shape volume. Instead, follow some simple rules until you are confident enough to know when you can break them.

Tips for Looking Slimmer

- Look for woven fabrics rather than clingy knits. Woven fabrics skim smoothly over your body, hiding any bulges; knits cling and reveal every frustrating bump.

- Dark colors are slimming, but light colors and white can be slimming also. Vertical stripes add to a longer, leaner look.

- Keep one basic color tone to your outfit—this will create a longer, leaner look.

- Make sure that you always buy clothes that fit well but never tight!

- Don't wear the new puffy styles thinking that you will hide beneath volumes of material. You won't. It will only make you look shorter and heavier.

- Select fabrics that are soft and thin—avoid heavy or bulky fabrics.

- Don't wear clothes with big details—no large bows, sleeves or lapels.

- Don't be a fashion victim. Before buying any of the new styles, check yourself in the full length mirror. If you don't have a "slim" silhouette, don't buy it.

Many of the suggestions in previous sections for small women and busty women hold true for you. If you follow the tips for short women on looking taller, you will look taller and consequently slimmer. If you look for the same types of fabrics and lines as the woman with the ample bustline you will also learn how to play down your figure.

The tactic of highlighting your strong feature works for your weight "liability" too. Divert attention to your face with gorgeous glowing skin and attractive makeup. Wear elegant earrings and necklaces. Look for a smashing hair style. Now is not the time to let depression over your weight problem affect your mental attitude. You have to be doubly conscious of projecting a confident and attractive image. Remember, others take their cue from you.

Are You Getting Better As You Get Older? Advice For The Mature Woman

In my visits to executive headquarters of corporations, I've observed a curious phenomenon. Older professional women seem to fall into two categories. The more successful look significantly better than their less successful counterparts. Do they look better because they are successful, or are they successful because they look better? Although there is no single answer, the difference is clearly not in the relative costs of their wardrobe and accessories. It is an overall look, and it comes from within.

In general, the successful women are more attractive and have mature but sophisticated styling. Their makeup enhances their looks but does not call attention to their age. Their clothes are chic and stylish. And they convey a sense of energy and fitness that belies their years. The less successful women, on the other hand, appear to have been defeated by age, and to have stopped caring or trying. Consequently, their age has become a liability rather than a badge of strong experience.

Whatever the "cause and effect" relationship, the plain fact is that if you are going to work in a corporation, your image is always going to be important. You can't sit back at 45 and feel that you can rest on your laurels. If you stop caring about how you look, you're giving out negative signals. You're telling the world you're tired and old. And even if you don't feel that way now, you will soon start to feel that way if you ignore your image.

Tips for Looking Just a Bit Younger

- Add some color and verve to your wardrobe. Now is the time when you can get away with softer, brighter colors without diminishing your authoritative appearance.

- Wear coordinates instead of matching suits. Mix fabrics and colors together for a stylish contemporary appearance.

- Look for softer styles in clothing rather than straight or severe lines.

- Use unusual, but quality, accessories.

- Get a soft, uplifting hairstyle. Long hair is out for the mature woman. In addition to dragging down the lines of your face and "aging" you, it says that you are not comfortable with your age.

- If you are starting to go grey, color your hair. (Greying hair on women is not nearly as flattering as it is on men.) More on this later in Chapter 12.

- Review the makeup colors you have been wearing. If you've had the same shade for several years, it may well be too bright for you now. Stick to softer tones, in all your makeup. Learn how to use a lipliner if you don't already know how. This will help keep the lipstick from running into lines and wrinkles around the lips.

- Pay strict attention to exercise and nutrition—it's now more important than ever. A taut toned body will go a long way toward a younger appearance.

Miracles of Modern Medicine—Plastic Surgery

If your skin is showing signs of significant aging and you're beginning to feel "old," consider plastic surgery. A skillful reputable surgeon can work wonders with aging skin. And there are a number of new, very simple procedures from which to choose.

But remember, a trip to the surgeon is not something to be taken lightly, nor am I advocating it for everyone. It's your face we are talking about, and it's the only one you have. But if you think that a slight change would improve your appearance, then consult a hospital or the board of plastic surgeons in your area for the name of a qualified surgeon. Always make sure the surgeon is Board Certified in plastic surgery. And check out his or her reputation, including a chat with some former patients. Investigate the pros and cons of the techniques you're considering. Only then, when you are quite sure, should you consent to any procedures.

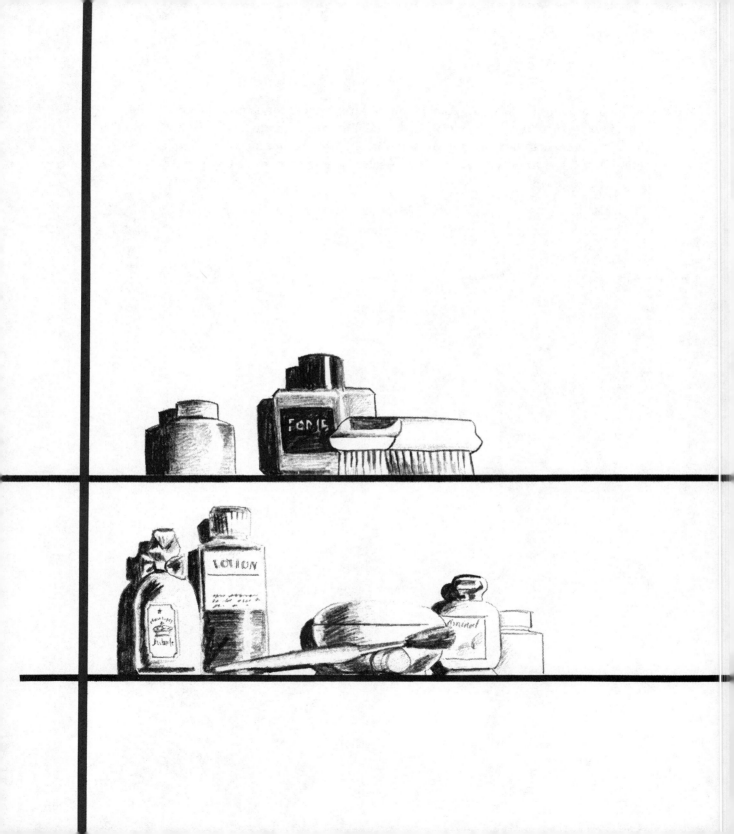

Chapter 10

Successful Skin
Facing Up to Your Image

At last the focus in the cosmetics industry has changed. For years, the major emphasis was on makeup and covering up the skin. Now, finally, it has turned to the health of the skin beneath the makeup.

It really should be obvious—your skin care is much more important than your makeup. If you have poor skin, no amount of makeup is really going to offset it—although the right makeup can bring out your best. Your goal should be to have the best skin you can—and that means it should be clear, smooth, and firm.

Some Bare Facts

Skin is skin. Not terribly profound, you may be thinking. But clinically, it is true. All of the skin on your body is the same. And the terms "dry," "oily," and "normal" skin are oversimplifications. There's really just underfunctioning skin, overfunctioning skin, and of course the kind we would all like to have—skin that functions normally.

- Underfunctioning skin does not produce enough protective substances (oils) to maintain the normal, internal moisture level of the skin necessary to keep it feeling comfortable and pliant. Hence, the term "dry" skin.

- Overfunctioning skin produces too much oil, which is forced out onto the surface of your skin creating a shine and other problems.

- If your skin is neither taut nor oily, then you have relatively normal functioning skin. Your skin provides just enough oil to keep it comfortable and dewy without excess.

Why Is It So Difficult To Get Good Advice?

The proper role of skin care is to compensate for your skin's improper functioning or to maintain its proper functioning. While it all sounds simple, and actually is, many women have problems with their skin that seriously affect their looks. Most of these problems stem from not knowing enough about skin. Many women rely upon salespeople at cosmetic counters to "prescribe" skin care programs for them. This can be the root of many problems!

Most cosmetics representatives have been trained in skin care by the cosmetic company for which they work to push high-profit products, or those that have excess inventories. Consequently, you are usually buying products that are good for the company but not necessarily good for you.

Enough of how you can go wrong in skin care. How do you go right? First, determine how your skin is functioning. Take the "Skin Functioning Test."

Skin Functioning Test

Remove all of your makeup. Check your skin in direct sunlight. Then take the test below and answer all three sets of questions.

Plus (+)

		Yes	No
1.	Does your skin develop a shine on your forehead, nose, or chin within several hours after washing?	___	___
2.	Do you have large pores?	___	___
3.	Do you have blackheads or whiteheads?	___	___
4.	Does your skin break out more than once a month?	___	___
5.	Does your skin break out in the outer cheek area?	___	___

Balanced (0)

		Yes	No
6.	Is your skin usually free of an oily shine, except possibly on your nose or forehead?	___	___
7.	Does your skin usually feel comfortable—no tight, dry feeling?	___	___
8.	Is your skin generally free of blemishes?	___	___
9.	Does your skin generally have a clear, healthy glow?	___	___

Minus (−)

		___	___
10.	Does your skin ever feel dry or tight?	___	___
11.	Do you have fine surface lines?	___	___
12.	Does it look dry—never a shine during the day?	___	___
13.	Is your skin free of enlarged pores and blackheads?	___	___
14.	Is your skin free from blemishes?	___	___

Scoring The Skin Functioning Test

Review the chart and see where you placed most of your checks.

If you answered mostly "yes" to the section labeled (+), then your skin has a tendency to produce too much oil.

If most of your positive responses were under (0), your skin functions normally.

And if most of your positive responses were under (−), your skin has a tendency toward dryness.

If you answered yes in two sections then your skin is a combination and must be treated accordingly.

Taking Care of Your Skin

Specific and detailed skin care programs are found at the end of this chapter. The procedures include the basics of taking care of your skin:

1. Cleansing and Exfoliating

2. Toning (for certain skin types only)

3. Moisturizing

4. Protecting

Extra
Edge

These should be done twice a day and should only involve a minimum of time.

Step I: Coming Clean

The most important step is thorough cleansing. The best cleansers for your skin are soap or water-soluble cleansers. When I mention soap, I am referring to the special skin soaps that are created specifically for individual skin types. Never use deodorant soaps, which can be extremely harsh, or perfume soaps, which can irritate the skin. Look for soaps that contain extra oils and emollients (superfatted) for dry to normal skin; antibacterial soap for oily skin; and moderate soap, such as a clay-based one, for normal skins.

Cleansers That Don't Clean

What's wrong with cleansing creams? These "tissue off" creams have soap as a base. When you spread the cream over your face and remove it with a tissue, you leave a film of soap on your skin. This film traps the dead skin cells that your skin constantly exfoliates (sloughs off). Much of the dirt and bacteria that was on your skin are now stuck in this soapy film. It's not a very pretty picture, and it's not going to give you very pretty skin either. Many women who use this type of cream have a grey, muddy cast to their skin. That's because their skin is not really clean.

Water Is Essential

Warm to hot water is excellent for your skin in a number of ways. It encourages your skin to slough off the top layer of dead skin cells, revealing smoother, healthier-looking skin beneath. The warmer the water, the more stimulation your capillaries will receive.

Contrary to what some so-called skin care "experts" will tell you, reasonably hot water will not break your capillaries. In fact, just the opposite is true. According to studies by dermatologists, hot water increases the flow of blood through the capillaries to the skin. This blood contains vital nutrients and when stimulated, brings these nutrients to all parts of your face and body. This helps you to maintain the elasticity and youthfulness of your skin.

Exfoliation—Shedding The Skin You're In

Your skin constantly sheds old cells and creates new ones. The top layer of your skin is composed of dead skin cells, which are removed when you wash. If they are regularly removed, your skin maintains a glowing, healthy look.

You can help to keep your skin looking clear and translucent by using a gentle scrub product, such as one of honey and almonds, in lieu of your cleanser once or twice a week. This encourages the exfoliation process when done in moderation. I do not recommend a buffing puff which is a piece of man-made fiber that you rub over your face.

Try substituting the scrub for a morning cleansing once a week if you have dry skin, twice if you have normal skin, and several times if you have very oily skin.

Exfoliation—Skin Sloughing Treatment for All Skin Types

1. Apply cleansing oil to eye and lip area.
2. In your palm, mix a scoop of your scrub (honey and almond) with some of your cleansing oil.
3. Apply scrub liberally over face except eye area. Leave on for 1 minute. Then with fingertips very gently rotate the scrub over face.
4. Rinse face well by splashing with warm/hot water. Pat dry.
5. Apply moisturizer—where skin requires it.

Step II: Toning

After you have thoroughly cleansed your skin, if you have any oily areas or areas of blackheads or blemishes you should apply a toning lotion to these areas only. The toning lotion should be a mild alcohol containing lotion. The alcohol will help to temporarily tighten the pores and remove any last traces of oil and bacteria.

If you have dry skin, with no areas of blackheads or oiliness, you should not use any toning lotion. And you don't need a non-alcohol freshener, either. The only purpose of a toner is to tighten pores and remove excess oils. Neither of which is a problem for dry skin.

Step III: Moisturizing

After you have cleansed and toned (if necessary) your skin, then you should apply a moisturizer. Apply it where your skin feels dry. If you have a tendency to produce an oily shine in certain areas, then your skin does not need any more oils in that area.

Generally the driest areas of a woman's face are around the eye area, the outer cheeks, the mouth and the neck. For the day you should use a fairly light moisturizer so that you don't have a "greasy" look to your face. If you prefer a thicker moisturizer at night, do so.

Moisturizers—Magic or Myth

More mystical properties have been attributed to moisturizers than any other product on the market ever, and virtually all of them are untrue! Moisturizers do not eliminate or prevent wrinkles and they don't sink deep into the skin to perform any other miracles.

Moisturizers can temporarily reduce the appearance of fine lines and wrinkles by plumping up the skin. They also provide a protective shield for your skin against the weather, and keep your skin feeling smooth, soft, and comfortable.

Moisturizers work in one of two ways. Either they trap moisture that's in your skin by forming a "shield" against moisture loss, or they have humectants, ingredients that attract the moisture in the air and then hold it in your skin. Some moisturizers do both.

Moisturizers differ although not to the extent that advertising campaigns would have you believe. The key difference is in the quality of the ingredients. Some contain less expensive oils which do not help retain moisture in the skin as well as some of the more expensive oils. There are no miracle ingredients, however, and there are no creams that can justify a $50 to $100 price tag.

Step IV: Protecting

The final step in your daily program should be to protect your skin. Your skin needs to be protected from the elements and the pollution. To protect your skin you should shield it with foundation and powder.

There are a number of misconceptions surrounding these items. Many women mistakenly think that they are being kind to their skin when they eliminate these items. They believe that their skin can "breathe" and their pores won't clog. They're wrong.

If you choose the right foundation and makeup, your skin should be able to breathe and your pores should not become clogged. On the plus side, your skin will look better and be protected. These products form a barrier between your skin and nature—they keep your skin from being dried out by the wind, prevent dirt and grit from clogging your pores, and filter out the harmful rays of the sun. Just as your clothes protect you from these elements, so do your foundation and powder.

I did say the right type of foundation and makeup. There are products which can give you problems. Avoid heavy, cakey or opaque foundations, since most skins need only a light foundation. I'll talk more about foundations and makeup in the next chapter.

Masques and Facials
In general, facials help to improve the appearance of your skin. If you have a tendency to break out or have blackheads and clogged pores, the esthetician can help to clean out your pores and reduce the breakouts. Your skin will appear much cleaner, softer and healthier, at least temporarily.

On the negative side, salons insist upon facial massages which are harmful to the skin. And almost always, they will push a plethora of moisturizers and oily, creamy products, regardless of your skin's actual needs. As I mentioned in the moisturizing section, moisturizers are big business and the most misused product in skin care. They are also responsible for most of the skin problems women have.

The Once-A-Month Superfacial for All Skin Types

This treatment, with some modifications, is based on facials given at some of the most expensive salons in the world.

1. Cover your hair with cap or towel.

2. Cleanse face. Do not apply any toner or moisturizer.

3. Add a mix of various dried herbs to a pan of boiling water and place pan on sturdy table.

4. Drape large towel over your head and keeping your face about five or six inches from pan, steam your face for about five minutes.

Extra
Edge

93

5. Pat face dry. If you have any clogged pores, clean them out. Cover your fingertips with pieces of tissue, and gently apply pressure to area around the blackhead or clogged pore. If the sebum does not come out easily, do not persist.

6. Dab an eye cream under eyes. Apply masque* over face except eye area. If it is a drying or hardening type apply several strips of wet tissue over the masque as you lie down. Soak two cotton pads in witch hazel and place over eye area. Relax for about ten minutes.

7. Remove masque with a warm, wet facecloth. Apply second masque. This should be a refreshing masque such as a chamomile masque. Relax for another ten minutes.

8. Remove masque by splashing face with warm/hot water.

9. Apply moisturizer. If skin is very oily or acned, add a touch of moisturizer only where skin is dry or tight.

Skin Preventive Medicine— Look Younger, Longer

There are a number of steps that you can take to keep your skin looking younger. The most important is to protect it from the sun. It has been proven conclusively that the sun damages your skin—its effects are cumulative and non-reversible. See *"Sun Sense"* in this chapter for some sound advice.

Sun Sense

Sun-Kissed Wrinkles

Your skin can be sun-damaged any time you're outside. And even by your late twenties and early thirties you will begin to notice the results—fine lines around the eye area, across your forehead, around your mouth.

The simplest and most effective way to prevent this fate and still enjoy the outdoors is to use a sunscreen. The best sunscreens use a combination of a PABA derivative and benzephenone. These two ingredients block out both types of the sun's ultraviolet rays—both of which can damage your skin.

Dry skin should use a moisturizing type of masque (such as a seaweed masque). Oily skins should use a drying masque (such as clay). Normal skins may prefer to use the clay type in the t-zone (forehead, nose and chin) and the moisturizing one on the rest of the face.

Sunscreens are now required to provide a protection number on their label (they typically range from 2 to 15). The higher the number, the more protection. A fifteen is usually considered a sun block—which allow no rays to penetrate the skin. I would advise using a minimum of a number 10 sunscreen if you feel that you still want to get some tan. It will take a while but you can feel happier that your tan won't be paid for in future wrinkles.

Another way to prevent sun damage is to always use your foundation and powder. They provide a protective layer on the skin that helps to filter out the sun's rays. Besides, it's once more fashionable to have pale, creamy skin.

Tanning Booths

Everything bad that I have just said about the sun holds true for sun tanning booths. Your skin is going to wrinkle and age faster if you use them. Don't let anyone tell you that these eliminate the "harmful" ultraviolet rays and only let in the "tanning" rays. It's just not true. Scientific evidence has proven that both types of rays cause sun damage and wrinkles.

The Pill and Your Skin

If you take an oral contraceptive your skin is also susceptible to increased sun damage. The most noticeable result is splotching of the skin due to excess pigmentation. A strong sunscreen or sunblock can help prevent this.

Smoke Gets in Your Eyes (and your skin)

You should be aware that smoking also affects the skin. Studies have shown that nicotine restricts the capillaries and blood vessels that bring nourishment to your skin particularly in the eye area. Smokers show a marked increase in lines and wrinkles around the eyes and the mouth. Research has also shown that smoking and sunbathing increases geometrically the amount of wrinkling and sun damage to your skin.

Skin Treatments for Looking Younger

While the precautions I cover in "Sun Sense" will help to slow down considerably the effects of aging on your skin, there are some treatments that you should consider when your skin begins to show its age. The current state of the art in all of these treatments is at a very high level and if approached with proper caution and evaluation, you should have no problems. There is nothing wrong or vain about wanting to look as good as you possibly can. It's a sign of a healthy ego, and it's human.

Collagen Injections

This is a relatively new treatment for age lines, scars, and wrinkles. It is performed in a physician's office and appears to be a safe procedure. Collagen is injected in a series of dots along a wrinkle or into the pit of a scar. There is minimal discomfort and after several treatments, the area beneath the line or pit is pushed up to become even with the surrounding skin. The wrinkle or pit disappears.

The results and the potential for this treatment are very exciting. You can eliminate many types of wrinkles and lines with this procedure without having to undergo the more serious operation of a face lift. If you have aging lines around your eyes, mouth or your forehead, consider this treatment. But remember, as with all procedures of this kind the results are temporary—lasting several years.

Face Lift

This is a much more serious approach to reducing the appearance of aging in your face. But if your face is showing significant signs of aging, it's a treatment worth investigating. With a reputable plastic surgeon there's minimal risk. Usually, however, the biggest problem with a face lift is in the mind of the patient. Many women expect miracles—and become depressed when they don't look twenty years younger. A good face lift will improve your appearance and make you appear healthier, brighter, refreshed and slightly younger.

A "lift" pulls and tightens the skin on your face which has "fallen" into loose folds. The procedure will not change the basic contour of your face. With good care the results should last anywhere from five to ten years. And it can be repeated successfully. If done well, you will never have the mask-like look that is often associated with repeated face lifts.

If you're considering a face lift, or any type of surgical operation, I strongly recommend that you research the plastic surgeon thoroughly. If he doesn't have time to discuss the operation and the results with you, or if he makes promises of regained youth, I suggest looking elsewhere. I also recommend having your face lift done in a hospital, as opposed to the new, in-the-office approach. While the operation is essentially safe, if anything should go wrong, it's better to be in a hospital.

Treatments to Avoid

Facial Massages (good for the psyche, bad for the skin)

Many books and skin care salons extol the virtues of facial massage and exercise. They claim that by toning the muscle under the skin, the skin will be firmed and toned. It's a nice theory, but, unfortunately, nothing could be further from the truth.

Think about it logically. There's an underlying structure of the skin containing collagen and elastin fibers, which hold the skin firm and smooth. Through age and sun damage these fibers are destroyed and the skin begins to sag and form folds (wrinkles). Pulling the skin, as in a massage, tears and deforms these support fibers. The damage is the same as that produced by the sun.

Facial Exercises

Facial exercise can cause wrinkles instead of preventing them. Think about where you get lines—around your eyes, your mouth, your forehead—all areas that experience the most movement. The habitual squinter or forehead wrinkler will sooner or later have lines around her eyes, or across her forehead. In other words, facial expressions and movements form lines. (Interestingly people who are incapable of forming facial expressions, such as catatonic mental patients, have fewer facial lines than normal). So with all of this in mind, who wants to indulge in facial exercises?

Silicone Injections

While exercise, massage, and the sun are bad for the skin, none can equal the havoc that can result from silicone injections, the injection of liquid, chemical material into facial lines. At one time silicone treatments were very popular. But as time passed and some silicone patients began to find unsightly and permanent bumps in the areas that had been treated, its general use was banned. Only a handful of surgeons are now allowed to use it, and their results are undocumented.

Silicone is not a natural substance and even under the best of circumstances and under the care of a reputable dermatologist things can go wrong.

Chemical Peels

This technique involves spreading a caustic solution on the face to burn away lined or acne-scarred skin. The mild peel burns away the top layer of skin, and the red, raw skin forms a crust in a few days. In about a week, the crust falls off leaving the skin firm and pink, and the lines and scars seemingly "eliminated." But this appearance is only because the skin is swollen due to the terrible assault on it by the chemicals. As soon as the swelling subsides (in a week or two) the skin looks as scarred and wrinkled as before.

In the deep peel, a solution (formed usually by a carbolic acid derivative and a cancer-producing drug) burns away the epidermis and the top layer of the dermis.

Extra
Edge

97

The skin is burned so severely that it swells considerably and a thick hard crust is formed. Patients are usually confined to bed for several days following this treatment. After 10 days or so the crust is peeled away, but the skin remains swollen, red, and sore. Once again the lines and wrinkles seem to have vanished. As soon as the swelling ceases (in this case about six months) they reappear.

These peels do not stimulate regrowth of firm young skin as many cosmeticians and even some doctors say. And the downside risks of this treatment are great, particularly if you are being treated by a cosmetician or a careless doctor. Because everyone has a different skin thickness and even areas of the same face differ, it is impossible to know exactly how much of these dangerous solutions to use. Consequently, scarring, hyperpigmentation (splotches of dark or light coloring on the skin), and even fatalities have resulted.

Unbalanced Dieting
Many women, in their attempts to lose weight, eliminate meat and other protein-containing foods from their diet. Before you take this route, you should be aware that protein is one of the best skin foods. It helps to keep the collagen substructure firm and young, which in turn keeps your skin firm and young.

Dry Skin Program

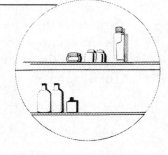

Cleansing products:
cleansing oil
water soluble cleanser
light moisturizer
concentrated moisturizer
eye cream

Specialty products:
moisturizing masque
honey/almond scrub

Morning Program
1. Splash very warm or slightly hot water over your face several times to get the skin prepped for cleansing.

*2. Apply cleanser and gently work up a lather.

3. Rinse well with slightly hot water at least six or seven times.

4. Gently pat skin dry.

5. Apply moisturizer immediately.

6. Proceed to makeup. Use a moisturizing foundation.

Substitute your scrub for cleanser once or twice a week in the morning.

Night Program

1. Remove eye makeup with cleansing oil.

2. Saturate fresh cotton ball with cleansing oil, and whisk over face to remove superficial makeup.

3. Follow steps 1–5 in the morning plan. If your skin feels very dry, you may wish to use a more concentrated moisturizer at night. Moisturize your neck also.

4. Gently dab eye cream around your eye area.

Mini Facial for Harried Exec—Dry Skin

1. Make sure face is cleansed properly.

2. Splash face six to eight times with hot water and apply a moisturizing masque over entire face, except eye area.

3. Dab an eye cream gently around eye area.

4. Leave masque on for ten minutes. Remove by splashing face with hot water. Gently blot cream from eye area.

5. Apply moisturizer immediately. If going out, proceed with makeup.

Normal/Combination Skin Care Program

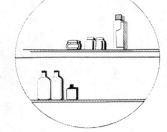

Cleansing products:
cleansing oil
mild soap or water soluble cleanser
mild alcohol-containing toner*
light moisturizer
eye cream

Specialty products:
clay masque
moisturizing masque
honey/almond scrub

Morning Plan

1. Splash face several times with hot water.

2. Apply cleanser and work up a good lather.

3. Rinse well by splashing face with hot water six or seven times.

4. Apply toner to any oily areas.

---

*only if you have oily areas

5. Apply a light moisturizer to face except oily areas.

6. Apply moisturizing foundation.

Night Program

1. Remove eye makeup with cleansing oil.

2. Cleanse face as in Morning Plan 1–3.

3. Apply toner to oily areas.

4. Apply moisturizer (more concentrated one at night, if necessary) to face except oily areas.

5. Dab eye cream around eye area.

Mini Facial for Harried Exec—Normal/Combination Skin

1. Cleanse face thoroughly.

2. Splash face with hot water six to eight times.

3. Apply a clay masque to face except eye area. You may wish to substitute a moisturizing masque in any dry areas.

4. Dab a concentrated eye cream around eye area.

5. Remove masque after ten minutes by splashing face with hot water. Blot cream from eye area.

6. Apply moisturizer immediately to all areas except where you have excess oil or blemishes.

7. If you are going out, proceed with makeup.

Oily/Blemished Skin Care Program

Cleansing products:
clay-based, or
   antibacterial soap
   (for blemishes)
alcohol-containing toner
oil-inhibiting night lotion
eye cream
light moisturizer

Specialty products:
clay masque
honey and almond scrub

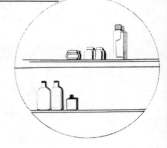

Morning Plan

1. Splash face several times with slightly hot water to prep it.
2. Apply cleanser and work up a good lather.
3. Rinse seven or eight times with slightly hot water.
4. Saturate cotton with toner and brush over oily areas lightly.
5. Apply light moisturizer to any areas where skin is dry.
6. Apply foundation. If your skin is very oily or blemished, use a water-base foundation.

Night Program

1. Remove eye makeup with cleansing oil.
2. Cleanse face as in Morning Plan 1–3.
3. Apply toner to oily areas. If you have excess oil or problem areas, try using an overnight oil-absorbing lotion on these areas only.
4. Gently dab eye cream under eye. Apply light moisturizer to any dry areas of skin.

Mini Facial for Harried Exec—Oily/Blemished Skin

1. Cleanse face thoroughly.
2. Splash face with warm water six to eight times.
3. Apply a clay masque to face except eye area.
4. Dab eye cream around eye area.
5. After ten minutes, remove masque by splashing face with hot water.
6. Apply toner to oily/blemished areas.
7. Apply moisturizer to any dry areas.

Extra
Edge

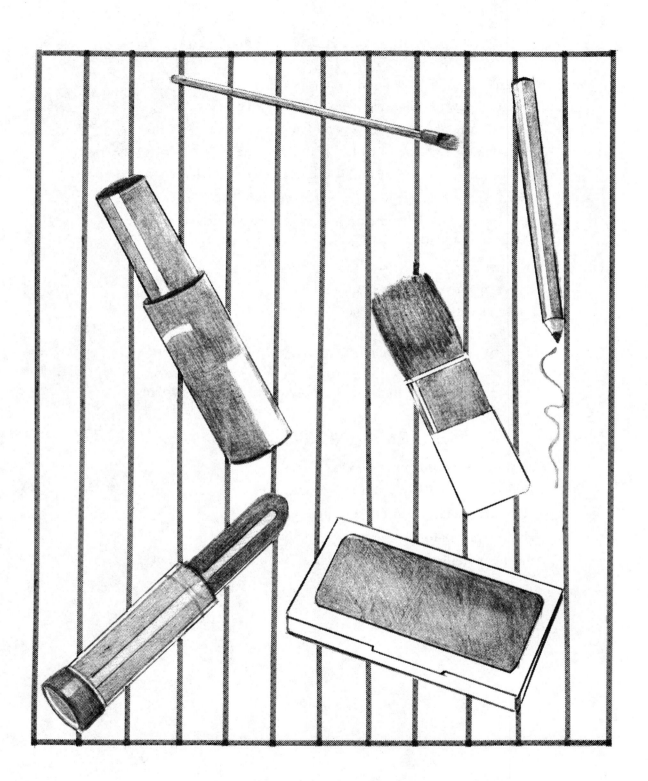

Chapter 11

Managerial Makeup

Color Me Professional

Makeup is an important part of a woman's professional image. The right makeup can create a cool, competent, and sophisticated look—one that says you have "grace under pressure." The wrong makeup can generate a lot of different impressions, none of them good. Until now the executive woman has had two choices in her makeup look—follow a well-known male authority on dress who advises "a touch of lipstick only, if you're under 35" or follow the beauty books that can have you made up to look like anything from a sultry siren to an innocent.

A professional woman should wear makeup. It makes you look more attractive, and as we have shown that's a definite plus in business. When done correctly, it completes your total image as a sophisticated, authoritative woman. And despite what you may believe, the right makeup is actually good for your skin.

Getting Started

I'll assume that, like most professional women, you have very little time in the morning. Before you begin, create a permanent makeup area—where you can

Extra
Edge

have a small table or a stand on which to keep all your makeup tools. You may not realize it now but these "tools" can help your makeup look better and save you time.

Putting makeup on in direct light will prevent you from putting too much on for daytime. If you set your table up near a window that gets direct light, you will get a softer daytime finish. While the fluorescent lighting at the office can drain makeup colors, many offices have areas of sunlight, too, and you don't ever want to appear harshly made up.

Once you have a makeup table set up, you'll need the following items:

Makeup Tools	Makeup
Professional large loose powder brush	Foundation
Professional blush brush	Loose face powder
Professional eyeshadow brush	Undereye cover
Combination eyebrow brush/comb	Blush
Makeup sponge	Mascara
Cotton balls	Eyeshadow
Tissues	Lip pencil
A face-size mirror	Lipstick
A headband	Eyeliner pencil

Put your headband on to keep your hair out of your face and then proceed with the following makeup plan.

Step By Step Approach To Managerial Makeup

1. Apply foundation. If you have normal/dry skin use an oil-based foundation and apply with a damp sponge. If you have oily or blemished skin use a water-based foundation and apply with a damp sponge.

You can apply your foundation with your fingertips or with a cotton ball, but for the best finish I suggest using a damp cosmetic sponge.

If you use a moisturizing foundation you can apply it to your undereye area. Or, if you prefer, use a lighter colored moisturizing undereye creme to hide dark circles.

If you use a water-base foundation, which has no oils, bring the foundation up to the top of your cheek, eliminating the undereye area. Then use a moisturizing undereye cover cream to keep the eye area moisturized. Make sure to blend well with your water-base foundation.

Never use foundation to add color to the face—not only does it look fake, it's unattractive. Your foundation color should match the color of the skin on the side of your neck or on your inner arm. You can get an even prettier "finish" for your skin if you go one shade lighter than your skin tone.

2. Apply blush color subtly. If you have normal or dry skin, use a cream blush and apply it to cheek area. If you have oily or blemished skin, use a powder blush and apply it with a professional powder or blush brush.

Make sure that you blend the blush well. Harsh lines of color create an over made up look that is very unprofessional. Professional brushes help to apply makeup subtly. The bigger the brush, the softer the color application.

The important thing to remember with cream blush is to apply it gently—never pull the skin or rub it harshly. It's better to apply too little than too much. You can always add more color.

If you have dry skin, a cream blush will help keep your skin moisturized. If you find that your blush seems to disappear within a few hours, you can "hold" it by applying powder blush (in the same color family) over the cream blush.

If your skin is oily or blemished, you should avoid cream blush since it adds unnecessary oils, increasing clogged pores or blemishes. A powder blush gives color while helping blot up excess oils.

If you have normal skin, you're free to use either the cream or powder blush, or you can use both for long-lasting color.

Extra
Edge

3. Apply loose powder over face and lip area with large powder brush.

Wait about ten seconds. Brush off excess powder. If you still have a powdery look, dab a damp (not wet) cotton ball over your face.

If your skin is very lined, double check your powder application to make sure the powder isn't caught in any lines. Dab these lined areas with a damp cotton ball. It's important to learn how to use powder since it helps to create a cool, flawless skin—perfect for a businesswoman.

You may have been told to apply powder first and then your blush. For your office look, using powder as the final step over blush gives your makeup a softer, more subtle finish and reduces any obvious color lines.

4. Brush-on Eyeshadow via one of the techniques below:

a. Apply one muted color (mauve, mocha, sand, grey, or slate) from eyelid to browline as shown.

b. Apply one muted color on eyelid and one highlighter shade (off-white, pale yellow, champagne, or soft pink) under the brow.

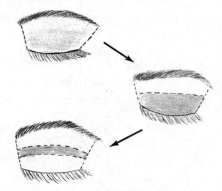

c. Apply one light color (off-white or pink) from eyelid to browline and then blend one of your deep muted colors (such as mocha) along the crease.

Experiment. Try a different technique on your day off. See which works well for you. Remember, if you are unsure about makeup, don't avoid it. Practice until you get the knack. After all, if business problems don't intimidate you, why should makeup?

5. Smudge a very soft eye pencil at outer corners of eyes.

For the most part you should use only soft black, slate, or brown eyeliner for work. Use just a touch of it at the outer corners of your eyes for emphasis. Don't rim your eyes with liner during the day; wait for night time. Bright colors such as loden, navy, and violet are too dramatic for the office.

Always test eyeliner pencils before you buy them. A good pencil should be able to draw a line on the back of your hand without applying pressure or moving the skin. If you have to press down on the pencil, if it scratches your skin, or if you have to move the skin, the pencil is not a good one. I recommend eye pencils instead of liquid liners, as they in general give a more appropriate look for the office. They are easier to work with, give a more subtle color, and can be smudged for a softer line.

Remember, the eye area is delicate, and daily pulling and pushing with an eye pencil can create lines. A common mistake women make in applying eyeliner is to stretch the skin taut around the eye so that they can apply the liner easily. Again, with the right pencil, this is unnecessary.

6. Add only one application of black mascara, to upper lashes.

For the office you really only need one application of mascara. Save that second coat for your night out on the town. Lash-Lengtheners aren't necessary—a quality, basic mascara is much more suitable for work.

Black is the most natural-looking mascara for most colorings. Surprisingly, brown seems more artificial, than black, except on the palest blondes.

If you have problems with smudged mascara underneath your eyes, avoid mascara on your lower lashes. Mascara is often moistened by the oils in makeup or undereye creams and then smudges onto your skin. You can't keep checking your mascara all day, so play it safe.

7. Line lips with a natural color pencil while they are powdered.

Use a soft pencil lipliner that has a color close to your natural lip color. Try an apricot shade. The color of your lipliner should never stand out from your lipstick.

Liner should never be obvious. Use it only to hold lipstick in place and to define your natural lipline. Don't attempt to increase the size or change the shape of your lips with a liner. You may be able to get away with a slight change at night, but in the office it will be obvious and very unprofessional.

8. Apply a matte lipstick to powdered, lined lips. Wait about 30 seconds and blot. Reapply lipstick.

You want your lip color to last as long as possible. By applying lipcolor to powdered lips, then blotting and reapplying, you will add hours to your color.

You should use softened earth tones instead of pale or bright pinks. Pink can give a number of different looks, from sweet and innocent to trendy, which

Extra
Edge

107

are not appropriate for the office. One makeup trick to soften the color of even the brightest or darkest lipstick is to apply a soft or "dusty" brown lipstick over the brighter lipstick. This softens any color.

While many women like the look and feel of high gloss lipstick or lip gloss, they are much too messy and unprofessional-looking for the office. Not only do glosses wear off quickly, they can easily smudge or smear your papers, or your clothes.

9. Brush your eyebrows into a neat arch.

If you have thin or light brows don't use an obvious pencil to fill them in during the daytime. Instead, brush some brown eyeshadow lightly over them. The eyeshadow will collect on the hairs and you'll have more natural-looking eyebrows.

If you have dark thick eyebrows, lucky you—they're in fashion now. But wild, uncontrolled brows are never in style. If they are difficult to keep in place, try a dab of hair spray and then brush them into place.

Don't pluck unless it is really necessary, and then try to limit your plucking to a few strays. Don't try to change your brows completely. If they are thick and dark you can balance your eye area by wearing deep, but subtle, eyeshadows.

Things That You Should Never Do for Office Makeup

- Use contouring colors. It can work at night, but for the office it's much too obvious and overdone.
- Wear metallic, sparkly, iridescent or shiny eyeshadows.
- Use bright shadows instead of earth tone colors.
- Wear any non-neutral color mascara such as blue, purple, or green.
- Apply several coats of mascara or worse, false eyelashes.
- Wear any bright eyeliner such as blue, green, or violet.
- Use liquid eyeliner instead of a soft smudged pencil liner.
- Wear iridescent face powder or blush.

- Line the inside of your lower lid with eyeliner. This is unwise as it can cause infection or inflammation of the eye.
- Use thick, gooey, lip glosses or glossy lipsticks.
- Wear obvious frosted lipsticks.
- Wear bright trendy colors such as fuchsia for lipstick or blush.

The Executive Touch-Up

No makeup look can last all day without a little touch-up. Especially if you've been running in and out of meetings all morning and are on your way to a business lunch. To handle these touch ups, you should set up a make-up kit for work. You can purchase a plastic organizer tray and set it up conveniently in one of your desk drawers. Then add the following items:

a good-sized hand mirror	a makeup sponge
a powder brush	nail polish remover
a blush brush	nail polish
an eyeshadow brush	nail file

Before you apply any makeup, it is important to have good light. If you have a windowed office, use the direct sunlight for touch-ups to prevent applying too much color. If you don't have a windowed office (and unfortunately in many corporations, windows are reserved for current superstars), you'll have to use the fluorescent lights.

Don't apply makeup looking into a large wall mirror with overhead fluorescent lighting. This can easily distort your makeup colors and intensities. Instead, use a good-sized hand mirror, and stand away from the lights, and let their reflection from one of the walls serve as your makeup light. This is a much better way to see what your makeup actually looks like.

Touch-Up Techniques

1. Remove lipstick with tissue.
2. Add more blush, only if it has disappeared.
3. Freshen up your face by applying pressed powder lightly with a large powder brush.
4. Line lips and apply lipstick to powdered lips. Wait, then blot. Reapply lipstick.

Extra
Edge

5. Lightly brush on more eyeshadow if color has faded or if lids are oily.

6. Add a touch of eyeliner to outer corners of eyes if it has faded.

Color Me Professional

There are two key areas to having a make-up look that is appropriate for the office. The first is how you apply the makeup. If you follow the guidelines I've presented, your makeup should give you an authoritative, attractive and completely professional look. The other part of a good office makeup depends on the colors that you choose. There are many colors available now that are pretty and fun—but dead wrong for the office. And it's often very difficult to get good advice in this area, since most women in cosmetics are unfamiliar with what is really acceptable in a corporate office.

You should basically stick with soft earth tones. They will give you a standard, crisp, mature look. And keep your face makeup balanced—have your eye makeup no darker than your lip and cheek makeup. Your eye and lip area should appear to have the same intensity of color. If you enjoy experimenting with different looks, try them on the weekends or at night. Don't use the latest makeup trends (such as pale lips with dark eyes, or the innocent pale pinks) in the office.

Winning Office Colors

	Color
Foundation:	Skintone or one shade lighter
Powder:	Translucent/skintone
Blush:	Plum/rose/mauve/mocha/tawny/beige
Eyeshadow:	Non-shiny colors: brown/plum/sand/slate/charcoal
Highlighter:	Non-shiny colors: soft white/pink/yellow/champagne
Lip Pencil:	Apricot/apple
Lipstick:	Plum/mauve/burgundy/berry/mocha/cinnamon/nutmeg/golden red/rose
Eye Pencil:	Slate/charcoal/dark brown/or soft black
Mascara:	Black/dark brown

Chapter 12

Starting
At
The Top—
Hairstyling That Works

For years women's hair kept them from doing many things. Going for a swim was a production; getting caught in the rain could ruin a night out. Many a spontaneous date was turned down because hair needed to be washed. In some respects a woman's hair kept her in her place as much as the ancient corset!

But beginning in the '60's, women began to look for styles and cuts that gave them more freedom. Today's plethora of styles and products reduce hair-care while increasing its natural attractiveness.

As a professional, your hair should always look attractive and well-cared for. It should be easily managed—you need a style that can look good for an important meeting or presentation at a moment's notice. It should withstand the elements and, with a quick brushing, look good again. You also need a style that will see you from an 8 a.m. staff meeting to an 8 p.m. dinner at an elegant restaurant.

Hair Styles That Work

A good hairstyle starts with a good cut. As a professional woman, you should be looking for a wash-and-wear cut. You need one that is so good that you really don't need to do anything more than wash, condition, and arrange it into the style you want. This is where your hairstylist comes into play. Don't skimp on your cut—get the best you can afford. If you need to cut expenses, eliminate the salon's blow dry or setting instead.

Step One: Interviewing Your Stylist

Select your stylist carefully. Ask women whose haircuts you admire what salon they use. Look in the newspaper for mention of stylists who are being interviewed or who may be styling hair for local fashion shows. If your city has its own magazine, look at the credits under the fashion photographs for the name of the hairstylist.

Once you have selected one or two promising stylists, set up time for a consultation. Ask to see the owner of the salon, who is usually the most experienced person. He or she should agree enthusiastically. If not, forget that salon. At the consultation, you should wear your typical work clothes and your regular hair style. This will help the stylist understand you and your "look." If you have a picture of a style that interests you, bring it. A good stylist will be able to tell you whether what you want is appropriate for your hair and your appearance.

Handling Service People

We should stop here for a minute to talk about dealing with service people. For some reason, many women who are in complete control in the office suddenly become intimidated by the hairdresser, the skin specialist, the salesperson in the clothing store. They find themselves being cajoled into a hairstyle, a makeover, or a dress that is completely inappropriate. This happens more often that we like to admit, and it is not an inconsequential matter. The wrong hairstyle can not only make you look unattractive, but can totally demoralize you and send your self-confidence spinning.

Just remember that you are in charge. Whether it is your makeup, your hairstyle, or your clothes, you must approach your objective as you would any other business matter. When you have the facts from the service person, YOU make the final decision. If the advice doesn't "feel right," don't take it.

The Consultation

Let's return to our discussion of the hairdresser. You should tell your stylist that because you are a professional woman, your hair style must meet certain requirements. It should be simple to care for—you don't have hours to wash, set, or whatever else some hairstyles require. And it should be attractive. (You don't have to sacrifice looks to get an easy-to-care for hair style). It should be softly controlled—in other words you shouldn't be afraid that your style will fall apart if you tilt your head or look down. If you are in the more conservative industries, it should not appear too trendy or different. And it should never flop in your eyes!

A good hairdresser will study your hair type and decide what style works well with it. The stylist should show an interest in your needs and your lifestyle. If not, forget it. And if the stylist claims to know best—or worse—that you are "stifling" his or her creativity, run! Twice, I have thrown caution to the wind and let the "artist" work. Both times I have regretted it.

Working Styles

There are countless hairstyles that will serve you well both at work and after hours. Illustrated in this chapter are sample styles for short, medium, and long hair—to get you thinking about your current hairstyle and some of the options you have if your style is outdated, too fussy, or simply too plain. I've said it before, but I will say it once more for emphasis—a professional woman should have an attractive hairstyle. Too many working women seem to feel that it's unprofessional to look attractive. As I've tried to show throughout this book, looking good can and should be used as a valuable asset to your career.

You will notice that I do not advise haircuts based on "face shape" or "texture of your hair" concepts. There are two reasons for this. Just as I don't think women should be packaged into uniforms, I don't believe that we should follow rigid rules that say certain face shapes require certain hairstyles. Wear what suits your individual personality and makes you feel your best. Second, thanks to modern techniques, you are no longer confined by the type of hair with which you were born. For example, if your hair is straight and you want a wavy style, you can get a permanent.

Shortcuts to The Top

A few years ago short hair meant "old-fashioned" or "masculine." Not any more! Some of the most contemporary and feminine looks involve short hair. These short styles are the easiest to care for of all styles. Most are wash-and-wear and

Extra
Edge

113

Styles that Succeed

Short hairstyles

If you have never tried short hair, consider it.
With the new cuts, short hair can give you a
surprising number of different "looks". Try bangs
one day and brush your hair all back and off your
face the next. Make sure that your stylist shows
you a number of different ways to wear your new
haircut.

can be freshened with a quick spray of water and setting lotion. The key difference in these short hair styles is in their soft, "full" look. And remember, if you opt for short hair, your choice of earrings becomes crucial. Use them to "finish" your look. (*See Chapter 8*).

If you're short, don't get a "little-boy" haircut—it can make you look too young or pixie-ish. If you're very tall, you should also avoid a very short haircut, which could make you look off-balance. This doesn't mean that you can't wear short hair, just don't choose an extreme style.

Middle of the Road

The second most easily managed hair length is medium. For most people, this is probably the most attractive length. Medium length offers the greatest versatility in styles.

Long

Professional women shouldn't have hair that falls below their shoulders. It's school-girlish, time-consuming, and outdated. Of course you can have long hair and pull it back in a bun or a pony-tail if you like, but it's usually not attractive on women past their twenties. And if you are only keeping your long hair because you feel that men find that length most attractive, do yourself a favor and cut it. Most men think they like long hair until you cut it—then they like the new length. (I've seen it happen over and over again).

If you want long hair, look for styles that just skim your shoulders. And look for a style that you can work in even if it's not pulled or secured back. The best styles are those that are shorter around your face and longer in the back. Some of the new styles even have short hair on top and around the face and sides. These styles give the effect of long hair while eliminating some of its problems.

How Often Should You Have Your Hair Cut?

There are some general rules to cutting hair. If you have short hair, you should have it trimmed about every six weeks. Upkeep is important because short hair very quickly loses its shape. Medium-length hair should be trimmed every two months. Shoulder-length hair needs trimming every two to three months. If your medium or long hair is layered, you should have it trimmed every six weeks because the shorter layers will start to flop. In the end, however, you are the best

Medium length styles

Many women look best in medium length hair. Look for a no-fuss style that gives you freedom.
Don't fight your hair. Have your stylist give you a cut that works with your hair.
Or consider a permanent if you want more wave. Get a style that gives you versatility, too.

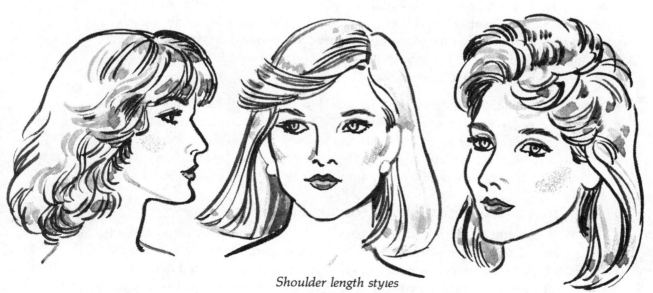

Shoulder length styles

As a professional woman, your hair should not fall below your shoulders—it can give you
an "ingenue" look that will work against you in business.
Make sure that your long hair doesn't overpower you. If you are short and prefer long hair,
experiment with some of the new styles that give the illusion of long hair without
the overpowering volume.

judge of when to cut your hair. You will probably notice before anyone else does that it's beginning to lose its shape or that it's harder to manage. That's the time for a haircut.

The Basics of Hair Care

Cleansing: The best care for your hair is frequent (even every day) washing in the shower. Contrary to popular belief, frequent shampooing will not dry out your hair. In fact it is very good for it. Just as you need to wash off the dirt and stimulate your skin through bathing or showering, you need to clean your hair and stimulate your scalp. After all, your hair goes wherever your body does—and it's exposed to just as much dirt and oil as your face is. A daily shampoo becomes even more important in big cities where pollution and grime are prevalent.

The shower is best for shampooing because you can usually rinse your hair better. If a film of shampoo or conditioner is left in your hair, it's going to lack body and look dull. If you do shampoo daily, one soaping is sufficient. And you don't have to be overly concerned with finding a shampoo that is pH balanced—most of today's products are.

If you have chemically treated hair, (straightened, permed, or colored) you should also stick to one soaping. Don't stop your daily shampoo just because you have had your hair color treated. In fact, the shampoo will help to wash out the heaviness of the color and make your hair look more natural.

Conditioning: If you use a hair dryer you should use an instant conditioner every time you wash your hair. People with oily hair that has not been chemically treated don't need to condition their hair after every shampoo—this can add to the oiliness. However, they should do so every second or third shampoo. If your hair has been chemically treated, you should use a conditioner after every washing.

It is, however, a good idea to use "deep" conditioners on occasion. Once a month is sufficient. Just as you don't give yourself a deep facial every week, you don't need deep conditioning weekly. In fact, consider combining your deep conditioning with your deep facial.

For best results, don't combine your haircare in one bottle—meaning don't use a combination shampoo/conditioner. Many of these shampoos are high in lanolin, which only coats your hair. And don't substitute a creme rinse for a conditioner—many of these products also add a slick of grease to the hair without conditioning the hair at all.

Hair Therapy

One technique for restoring life and luster to hair that I strongly recommend is the Hot Oil Treatment. While many exclusive hair salons provide this service for their clients, you can do it very simply at home and save yourself both expense and time. Try it once a month. You'll definitely notice the results.

1. Heat olive oil—approximately ½ cup for long hair, ¼ cup for shorter hair.

2. Dip cotton ball into the oil and begin to apply it to your hair—starting with the ends as they receive the fewest protective secretions from the scalp.

3. When the hair is saturated with the oil, wrap plastic wrap around your head.

4. Sit in the sun or under a hairdryer for 10–15 minutes, then remove the plastic. You can keep it on overnight by using a shower cap over the wrap.

5. Shampoo hair. Soap twice. Do not rinse hair before shampooing.

Special Treatments—Haircoloring

As you approach your thirtieth birthday, you may notice that your hair lacks the intensity of color or shine that it had when you were younger. It's not necessarily grey, just duller and drabber. It may not be noticeable to other people, but you can see it. Unfortunately, it's not your shampoo or your conditioning—it's the natural aging process that usually precedes greying. While it isn't significant enough to send you to the salon for a new color, you don't have to accept it, either.

One company has developed a unique product that has been designed to restore your hair's vitality without changing its natural color. It's not a permanent color change, but it will last through six or more shampoos.

Semi-Permanent Color

Once you actually have some grey, try semi-permanent products. For the best results, choose a shade that is one shade lighter than your present hair color. This won't change your natural hair color but the grey will take on the lighter shade and be unnoticeable. For example, if you have medium brown hair with a slight amount of greying, and you use a light brown shade, the treatment will not change the overall color of your hair. But the grey strands will turn light brown, which will give a soft, attractive, highlighting effect to your hair.

For haircoloring that lasts until the hair grows out, use permanent haircoloring. This type of product gives you the ability to go darker or lighter. In contrast, the semi-permanent colors will not lighten your hair. Permanent colors thus enable you to choose any color hair you want.

Over-the-counter products will give you results equivalent to those of any hair salon. There have been significant improvements in these products over the last ten years and procedures have been simplified. It no longer takes hours to change your color, nor is it messy. It is now possible to get the haircolor you want easily and professionally.

If you want to change your overall color, do it. Try gradual changes shade by shade. Drastic change could have a shock effect on your co-workers and could make you appear a trifle flighty, which is the last thing a professional woman wants. I don't recommend experimenting frequently with different colors. A business associate of mine was talking about one of the women at her company who had recently been fired. Part of her description was, "Well, she was a bit flaky—you never knew what color hair she would have from month to month." That's hardly a ringing endorsement for a manager.

This caveat aside, every woman over thirty should consider one or another of the techniques I've discussed. There is no reason to have drab, lifeless color, unflattering grey, or any dissatisfaction with your natural hair color. Remember, anything that makes you look and feel better about yourself is good for your professional image.

Other Special Treatments—Chemical Hair Control

With the advances made in permanents and straighteners, there is no need to be a slave to your hair. If your hair is straight and you would like a slight wave without using hot rollers every morning, you can now have it. If you prefer a curlier look, that's possible too. Or if your hair is too wavy and out of control, you can now have more manageable hair within an hour. While many of the old products were harmful to your hair and often unpredictable, today's products are superior in both quality and the ease of use.

Extra
Edge

Making Waves

If you like the look of wavy or curly hair, but you hate having to set your hair constantly to get it, consider having a permanent. All you have to do then is shampoo, towel dry, and run your fingers through your hair to bring out the wave or curl. You don't have to worry about setting your hair before you go out after work, or watching your set droop in the humidity, or not looking your best at work because you just didn't have time that morning to set your hair.

I recommend that you have your first permanent at a good hair salon. Consult with the hairdresser about the type of hair you have and the style that would be best for you. Perhaps you need a body wave, or a curly wave to give you the look you want. Then watch as your hairdresser gives you the permanent and ask questions. Consider it a learning experience so that next time you can perm your hair at home at your convenience.

A body wave will make fine, limp hair look and feel thicker. Your hair will move with you instead of clinging lifelessly to your head. It will also make coarse, wiry hair more manageable. Body waves work well on either one length hair or hair that's slightly layered.

A curly wave is similar to a body wave, only curlier. The amount of curl depends upon the size and number of rollers that you use—fewer, bigger rollers give a softer curl, while more numerous, smaller rollers give a tighter curl. Small rollers work well on a layered cut to emphasize the curl.

If you prefer to try do-it-yourself permanents, start with a body wave. This makes only a slight change in your hair, but it will give you time to adjust to a new look. You can feel comfortable walking into work the next day, and people will only notice that you look better. Then if you enjoy the look and the freedom, stay with the body wave. If you find you like the wave but want to go to a curlier style, move on to the next step. A good perm will last from three to six months, depending upon the type of perm and your hair. As your perm grows out be sure to have your hair shaped so that it will always look its best.

If you have a color-treated hair, you should only use products designed for color-treated hair. This will lessen the chance of damaging your hair. Obviously, before you try another chemical treatment, make sure your hair is in good condition. And use conditioning treatments often. You should wait at least a week after coloring your hair before perming it.

Straightening

If your hair is so curly and frizzy that it is really impossible to manage, consider straightening it. While I can wholeheartedly recommend perms, I recommend straightening with reservations. Done properly, with only a mild straightening solution, it will eliminate more than half of the curl and yet allow your hair to still retain body and bounce. However, if done incorrectly, it can cause considerable damage to your hair.

For this reason, I strongly recommend having your hair straightened by professionals at a reputable hair salon. Make sure that the hairdresser tests the solution on a few strands of your hair before applying it. You should start with a very mild straightening solution and see if it gives you the manageability that you need. Remember—the stronger the solution, the drier your hair will become.

Some Tools of The Trade—Useful Appliances

Blow Dryers: While I favor wash-and-wear hairstyles, if you have a style that you feel very good in but that requires blow drying, you should know which is the best dryer for you. Look for one that has at least several different heat settings. This will enable you to control the amount of heat and curl that you get. The lower the setting the better for your hair, although it will take a while to dry long hair. If you travel a lot, look for one that is compact or that folds. If you travel to Europe often, get one with European current adaptability.

If you have a wavy or curly style, try using a blow dryer with a diffuser. A diffuser looks somewhat like a flat shower head and it slips over the nozzle of your dryer. It "diffuses" the air and helps to bring out the curl or wave in your hair instead of straightening it as ordinary blow dryers do.

Styling Comb: A styling comb is similar to a curling iron except that it has teeth. You can use it in place of your brush and blow dryer. A styling comb will give you a soft style without lumps, bumps, or ridges. It's especially convenient to use when you travel or simply need a quick touch up.

Infrared Lamps: You can purchase an infrared bulb at your local hardware store and use it in any light socket in your home. I found one of the most convenient ways to use it is in a flexible desk lamp which can turn to any angle. The infrared lamp is perfect for hair with some wave and a wash-and-wear cut. While your hair is still wet, simply dab on some setting lotion and finger-style the look you want. Add a few clips if necessary to hold the style in place. Then just sit back and relax. This is also the least damaging method of drying your hair—next to letting it dry naturally.

Electric Rollers: These can be very handy for the working woman. When you need a quick set, just use these and in a few minutes your hair will be curled. Use them for last-minute emergencies or when you are traveling. I would not use these on a daily basis, though, because they can dry your hair.

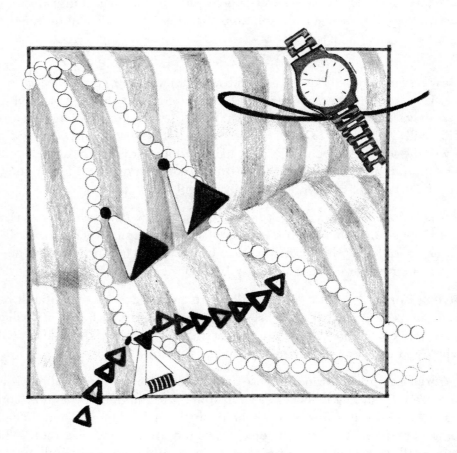

Chapter 13

Speaking of Business—

The Management Communications Game

Did you know that every time you speak or write a memo you say more than you may realize about yourself? How you phrase things, the way you write, your vocabulary, and your pronunciation all give signals to other people. The way you communicate may tell the listener that you are unsure of yourself, that you are nervous, that you feel subordinate, or even that you lack some of the finer points of education.

Managerial Voice Impact

If you think that a voice can't make or break a career, remember John Gilbert. He was one of the biggest stars of silent films—but he became a has-been overnight with the advent of the talkies. Gilbert was one of many stars whose voice failed to live up to the image created on screen. As an executive, your voice is also important to your career.

Some women have soft, high-pitched voices that lack authority. Alyson had been brought up to speak softly and converse politely because it was the "proper and ladylike" way for a young woman to behave. But during business meetings, she often found herself in a losing battle to get the attention of those at the table. All too often her soft voice would be overshadowed by a louder, deeper (and male) voice. Although her politeness had served her well in her social life, it was now a hindrance.

Other women entering the corporate world feel that they must adopt a "masculine" tone, which often comes across as shouting. Marcia, who was aware of the drawbacks of a soft, demure voice, was determined to project a tone of authority. So she adopted a "macho" style of tough talk with an overly loud voice. Unfortunately, her overcompensation generated behind-the-scenes ridicule from her associates, rather than the respect she desired.

A man's voice is generally a positive factor in his image. Usually strong and deep, it conveys a sense of confidence and authority. Some women's voices, however, can be strongly negative. From childhood on, they have subconsciously used their voice to play roles, particularly that of the "helpless" female. Some have also developed other so-called "girlish" traits such as giggling, speaking in "soft, ladylike" tones, shrieking with excitement, and whining—none of which is acceptable in the corporate world.

If you find at meetings that someone can grab the spotlight from you even while you are speaking, if you have difficulty getting a group's attention, if people appear preoccupied while you are talking, or if they ask you to repeat what you have said, chances are good that you need to develop voice impact.

Does Your Language Label You a Loser?

Many women have difficulty in giving commands, particularly to male subordinates. They have been brought up to speak deferentially to men and believe (subconsciously) that the man is to have the last word. When their role is reversed and they become the authority figure, they become uncomfortable. Consequently, they preface their directions with so many apologies that subordinates not only feel the assignments are relatively unimportant, but begin to lose respect for them as business managers.

Margaret is a recently promoted financial manager who supervises one analyst. "I would ask him to hurry up on a project by saying, 'Gee, I really would like to see you put more attention on the budget reports if you get a chance,' because I wouldn't want to be rude. Then I couldn't figure out why he wouldn't do what I wanted and would continue to work on some other project. Now I say what I mean and give specific directions without dancing around the point. The results have been dramatic."

Some women seem to have problems when they want to contribute an idea, particularly at meetings. Their ideas are preceded by an apology ("I don't mean to interrupt, but I had an idea . . .") or a profession of relative ignorance on the subject ("I'm not an expert on this subject, but . . .") or self-criticism of their forthcoming idea ("This probably won't work, but . . ."). Most of these problems can be traced to an upbringing that discouraged "aggressive" behavior in women, and all of it can negatively affect your image in business.

The Corporate Coup de Grace—The Presentation

Probably the most threatening area of communication for many people is public speaking. Some of the most powerful executives in the world still experience stage fright before addressing a large audience. But they manage to conquer their fear by the time they get to the podium.

Other younger and inexperienced managers may find that their image takes a nose dive after each oral presentation. As Ann, a management consultant, put it, "I started out in consulting with a hot-shot group and things looked promising for me. We tackled several interesting assignments and I had a major role in developing the written material for the proposals. While the final oral presentations to the clients were handled by my boss, I was assigned one area to present. That's when my troubles began. Even thought I knew the facts cold, I clutched during my speech and my boss had to jump in. While I did recover, I knew I had suffered a loss of credibility."

What Hidden Messages Does Your Voice Convey?

As a managerial woman you should be very aware of your voice and of any areas that may need improvement. We have found that many women are unaware of how they actually sound and are not using their voice to enhance their Total Professional Style. Through simple exercises and other techniques you can develop a speaking style that commands attention and conveys a strong sense of self-confidence. The first step for self improvement is to get an idea of how you sound now. Take the "Managerial Voice Test."

The Managerial Voice Test

Get a tape recorder, and an inexpensive telephone adaptor. Any cassette type recorder of reasonable sound quality will do. Tape yourself in a number of different situations, preferably in a way that will make you forget that you are recording what you say. Try:

A. Talking informally with a friend.

B. Reading a memo or taking part in a business meeting.

C. Conducting a business call with a friendly associate or someone with whom you feel powerful.

D. Conducting a business call with an intimidating adversary. In fact, the more difficult the conversation, the better.

Listen first to your conversation with a friend. This gives you an idea of what your normal conversational tone is, without the effects of stress and tension.

Then listen to the other conversations, and ask yourself these questions.

Section 1. The Sound of Your Voice

	Yes	No
1. Is your voice high-pitched?	____	____
2. Do you have to strain to hear every word?	____	____
3. Did it sound as if you were yelling?	____	____
4. Do you sound girlish?	____	____
5. Do you sound tough?	____	____
6. Is your voice harsh or unpleasant?	____	____
7. Does your voice reflect confidence?	____	____
8. Does your voice strain or break?	____	____
9. Do you sound relaxed?	____	____

Section 2. Tactics

	Yes	No
10. Did you lead the conversation, rather than just respond to others?	____	____
11. Were you expressive, effectively emphasizing important points?	____	____

	Yes	No

12. Did you enunciate your words properly? _____ _____

13. Did you say "umm" or "you know?" _____ _____

14. Do you drop off word endings, e.g., laughin', or jumpin'? _____ _____

Section 3. Your Words

15. Do you mispronounce words? _____ _____

16. Do you use slang? Or phrases such as "... like, you know"? _____ _____

17. Do you use cliches? _____ _____

18. Do you make grammatical errors? _____ _____

19. Do you use the same words over and over again? _____ _____

Section 4. Oral Presentations

20. Do you sound stilted or rehearsed? _____ _____

21. Does your presentation voice sound different from your conversation voice? _____ _____

22. Do you use pauses effectively? _____ _____

23. Do you speak too quickly? _____ _____

24. Do you vary your speaking speed as your intended effects vary? _____ _____

Answers & Scoring

Section I. YES 7, 9; NO 1–6, 8
Section II. YES 10–12; NO 13, 14
Section III. NO 15–19
Section IV. YES 22, 24; NO 20, 21, 23

Give yourself one point for every correct answer; zero points for every incorrect answer. In each section, determine the percentage of correct answers. A score of less than 75 percent in any particular category indicates a problem area that requires attention.

Extra
Edge

Section	# correct	# questions	% correct
Section 1. The Sound of Your Voice		14	
Section 2. Tactics		5	
Section 3. Your Words		5	
Section 4. Oral Presentations		5	

Your Natural Voice Is Your Best Voice

Now that you have heard yourself in a number of different situations and have reviewed the previous questions, let's discuss some ways to develop voice impact. It may surprise you to know that your natural voice, with its normal pauses and emphasis, is generally your best speaking voice. When people are relaxed and comfortable their voices are usually lower than when they are emotional. You may have noticed the difference in your voice as you conducted the different parts of the test.

Finding Your Natural Voice

Find your natural voice. With your tape recorder on, select a passage of text from one of your magazines on a familiar subject. Practice reading it a few times so that you know the overall point of the passage. Then:

1. Sitting comfortably, breathe deeply several times.

2. Close your eyes and slowly rotate your head in a complete circle to relax your muscles.

3. Now that you are relaxed, begin to read. Don't hurry; take your time and speak from as deeply within your body as is comfortably possible.

4. Pause at ends of sentence and paragraphs for breathing. Enunciate each word.

Now listen again to the tape. If you followed the directions, you will hear how your voice sounds when you are free from stress and tension. Emotions can cause your voice to hit a higher than normal pitch, an effect that is not especially important or noticeable in men, but that can sound unpleasant or strident in women.

If you feel that your voice is still too high, relax once more and concentrate for a few seconds on how low and relaxed your voice can sound. As you are thinking about a low voice coming from way inside your body, read the text once more.

You should find that your voice sounds lower. For a few weeks, try to be more conscious of your voice when you are speaking. And think "low" and "relaxed." You should soon have a lower, more vibrant speaking voice.

Speaking of Business

As an executive woman you should strive to have a voice that not only sounds pleasant but also conveys a cultured, educated background. And just because you have a college or a graduate degree, don't assume that you sound as if you do. Many well-educated people speak poorly. Proper speech requires constant awareness of vocabulary and grammar in addition to accuracy of pronunciation. Many people just become lazy and neglect their speech once they have passed English grammar class.

Just to start you thinking about your own speech:

Do you ever say: Incorrect	When you should say: Correct
"If I was her . . ."	"If I were she . . ."
"Are you inferring that I . . ."	"Are you implying that I . . ."
"I could of . . ."	"I could have . . ."
"I'm heavier than her."	"I'm heavier than she."
"Just between you and I."	"Just between you and me."
"This impacted favorably on sales."	"The impact on sales was favorable."
"Irregardless of what they said,"	"Regardless of what they said,"

Or, how do you pronounce the following words:

	Incorrect	Correct
jewelry	joo-le-ree	jew-el-ree
irrevocable	ir-re-voke-a-ble	ir-rev-a-ka-ble
harass	ha-rus	hu-rass
granted	gran-it	gran-ted

Another embarrassing and often amusing error is the "dangling participle": "Working diligently, the memo was completed on time." (The memo didn't work diligently, you did!)

You can easily improve your grammar and word power. Get a high school grammar text and test yourself. Work on those areas in which you need help. Use a thesaurus and a dictionary whenever you write or read. It's a painless way to expand your vocabulary. And don't make the mistake of thinking that it is unimportant. Many people (possibly even your boss) are quite surprised when someone supposedly well-educated uses incorrect grammar.

On Becoming a Corporate Cicero

One last word on an important aspect of corporate communications—speaking before an audience. Many people experience nervousness and "opening night" jitters before they make a public speech or presentation. The passage of time should reduce your stage fright, but there are some things that you can do now to become a more effective public speaker.

First of all, understand that you are not alone. You are not the only one whose mouth gets dry, whose palms become sweaty, and whose feet want to make a mad dash in the opposite direction of the audience. We've all experienced it. But you can learn to channel that adrenalin into a positive force.

If you are not prepared for your speech, then you have a right to be nervous. But I'll assume that you are well-versed in your subject and have prepared an effective presentation. If you are, the following suggestions should help you become more relaxed.

Preparation
Have a "dress rehearsal" of your presentation, if possible, in the room where you will be speaking.

- Do not memorize your speech—you may sound stilted and rushed, and forgetting one thing can destroy your entire presentation.

- Learn to pause between important ideas—you can gather your thoughts while giving the audience time to assimilate your views.

- Outline your speech, hitting the key points in the order in which you want to make them.

- Memorize the outline, or have it on a small card.

- Try not to use excessive notes—they hinder spontaneity and naturalness and cast doubts on your ability and knowledge.

Again, your trusty tape recorder is a valuable tool. Tape your rehearsal and review it. Does your speech still have punch? Does it flow logically? Does it interest you? Or do you rush through it in half the time you planned?

Before your presentation
Sit quietly and repeat to yourself several times that you are prepared and that you have some interesting information for your audience. Remember that the audience is not there to judge you, but to learn from you. And with a little practice, anyone can be an impressive speaker. (Remember that most people make incredibly dull and rambling speeches that bore everyone. Your practice has already given you a major advantage).

"The Pen Is Mightier . . ."/Managerial Word Power

The written word is closely related to the spoken word. In terms of the beginning executive's career, writing is even more important than speaking. Upper management generally will see your written work long before they ever meet you. And to many of your business contacts, you are what you write. Your choice of words and grammar can enhance or ruin your image-building process.

If you think that your company doesn't care how you say what you mean, think again. Lack of adequate writing skills leads the list of complaints against business school graduates by personnel executives, and most major business schools have made significant efforts in recent years to improve their writing training programs.

One company for which I worked placed an almost fanatical emphasis on writing style. It was management's belief that if you couldn't write logically, you couldn't think logically. "A sloppy memo denotes a sloppy mind." Everyone, from the lowest brand assistant to the division manager, spent weeks reviewing and rewriting memos to ensure that there were no misspellings, no ill-chosen words, no incorrect grammar. To some people, this may seem to be a waste of time, but, Procter & Gamble is one of the most successful companies in the world!

Writing memos is a valuable learning device as well as an important part of your career. The process helps you think clearly, analyze business problems, and draw logical conclusions. If you master business writing, you will enhance your stature in the corporation—as a manager who is effective in communicating her ideas and getting things accomplished.

The key to writing effectively is planning and organization. That shouldn't be surprising since anything well done needs to be planned carefully and organized in

Extra
Edge

detail. This is particularly true in business writing. You cannot sit down at your desk and begin to write in a stream-of-consciousness fashion. In fact, once you have done the necessary research and outlined your memo, the actual writing should take very little time.

Developing Your Memo

Before You Write . . . *Prepare:*

- Determine who your reader is and what action you want the reader to take.

- Define what key factors your reader will want to consider in making a decision. Avoid superfluous factors, tell the reader only what is pertinent to this specific decision.

- Gather all the necessary information relating to the key factors. Learn all you can about your proposal, then sort and discard irrelevant material.

- Review the information and draw logical conclusions. It's your job to analyze your material and interpret it for the reader.

After you have done all the research . . . *Outline*

- Jot down on the page, in any order, your ideas.

- Once you have this random list in front of you, you can then begin to organize the ideas intelligently.

- Use the "Inverted Pyramid" model to organize your thoughts. In this approach information is presented in decreasing order of importance.

Finally . . . *review* your outline to ensure that it:

- Includes a clear and complete statement of your purpose.

- Provides sufficient background data for evaluation.

- Presents conclusions, reasons, findings briefly and in order of importance.

- Includes necessary supporting data in the body or exhibits.

"Write" to the Top

Once you are completely satisfied with your research, preparation, and your outline, then begin to write. Your first paragraph is worth almost as much attention as the rest of your memo combined. This is your opportunity to telegraph to others exactly what you are asking of them. The first paragraph should answer the following questions: "What is being recommended?"; What key details influence this decision?"; What other departments or people are in agreement or what agreements are still needed?" What decisions are needed at this time?"

Then give your recommendation in detail. What are you recommending? How is it to be accomplished? What key considerations must be kept in mind? Discuss each reason for your recommendation in order of its importance.

The "Write" Choice

Simplicity, clarity and precision are key in selecting words. Use words which express the exact meaning you wish to convey. This does not restrict you to one-syllable words. But it should preclude you from using words that are stilted, ambiguous or lofty. As you write:

- choose short words over long
- select the familiar and concrete over the unfamiliar or abstract
- be precise instead of general
- use the active voice over the passive voice

And finally, edit. Edit your proposal at least two or three times before you forward it. Review each word—if it doesn't contribute to the memo, delete it. Review each sentence and each paragraph. Does the memo say exactly what you want to say? Leave your memo overnight and review it again the next day.

The "Write" Look

A well-written memo will look inviting. It should have wide margins with plenty of space in between the different elements. White space makes a memo inviting to read. Avoid a memo which crowds the sheet and is loaded with type.

Does the memo have eye appeal? Does it look easy to read? If not, you may lose your readers before they even begin. Are there too many long paragraphs? Do you use headings to capsule your information? Can you pick out the major points easily?

Your memo should also be mechanically perfect. Make sure that there are no typos, no misspellings, no inappropriate words or faulty grammar. Remember your memo is the packaging for your ideas. A "perfect" memo signals to the reader how important the idea is to you. It also demonstrates how much you value your reader's attention.

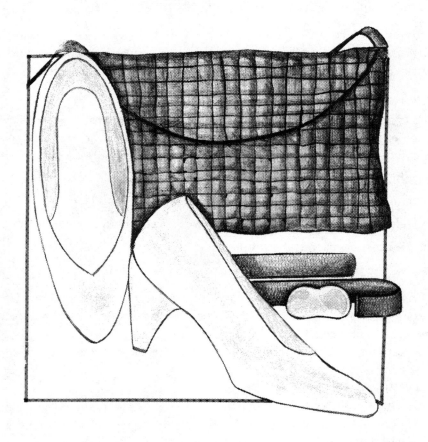

Chapter 14

The Corporate Body—
Games Working Women Play

You may be surprised to find a section on health and fitness in a book focusing on career success. But there are several good reasons why even a busy executive woman should take the time to be physically fit. As executives from some of the country's major corporations are discovering, corporate exercise programs lead to healthier, happier and more productive employees.

HARVARD STUDY QUESTION

How important is a woman's level of physical fitness as a career factor?

Seventy percent of the Harvard respondents said that a woman's physical condition was "somewhat important" or "very important" as a career factor. Cited was the fact that physical fitness was an effective way to deal with job stress, and that a fit and trim appearance was a

Extra
Edge

positive factor in a professional's image. While recognizing the importance of fitness, many women expressed concern about finding the time for an exercise program.

"Wellness"

Physical fitness comprises but one part of the general concept of what health experts now call "wellness." The others are stress management, nutrition, and medical self-care. All are important and relevant to the executive woman. Stress is an unavoidable part of her daily routine. And as far as nutrition is concerned, the managerial woman often has to "make do" with fast food preparations for lunch, and at the end of the day simply grabbing a quick meal and collapsing on the couch.

We asked several experts at Harvard University for realistic suggestions on exercise and nutrition for the working woman. We wanted a program that could be incorporated into your schedule and not someone else's; exercises for the office when you really can't get your exercise any other way; and ways to eat better whether you are "brown bagging" it or taking a client to lunch.

The Fitness 3: The Basics of a Good Executive Exercise Program

Before you set up your personal exercise plan, you should have a good understanding of what constitutes a relevant and useful program. The Harvard experts believe that the best exercise program is one that includes activities that work on the three key areas of physical fitness:

1. Cardiovascular
2. Flexibility
3. Muscle System

Balance is of paramount importance. Unknowingly concentrating your efforts in any one area can prove not only unproductive, but downright dangerous. For example, take the woman who is determined to start jogging. She has no previous running experience and starts running a mile a day to "get in shape." While this activity may immediately benefit her cardiovascular system, her new activity may be very harmful to her joints. The predictable result is "burn-out." You know what that means—she simply quits exercising after the first few times because the consequences are just too unpleasant. So much for that physical fitness plan!

Before Starting Your Program

Before you undertake any exercise program, you should follow these recommendations:

1. If you are over 35, get a complete physical checkup. For the best advice, look for one of the many doctors who now specialize in sports medicine. Have a basic exercise program planned in advance, and discuss it with your doctor. If he/she sets limits, follow them.

2. Start slowly and build gradually. *Progression* is the key word at all times. If you overextend yourself in the beginning, you can get hurt. Listen to your body; it will tell you when you have pushed too much. Pain does not mean results!

3. Don't be discouraged if you don't see immediate results. If you are in your twenties and have been minimally active, you will probably be able to get in shape within a month. If you are in your thirties or forties and have "let yourself go" for a number of years, it may take several months before the results show. But if you stick with it, it will be worth it.

4. Look for activities that you enjoy, that are fun. This will make your exercise program seem like more of a treat than a chore. Make exercise a social activity—go to classes or have a regular routine with a friend.

5. Leave the competitive and aggressive spirit at work. Don't overdo your exercise program because you feel the need to "win" at everything you do.

Fitness Formula—How to Personalize Your Own Program

Instead of following someone else's fitness program, develop your own. After all, you know best what activities you enjoy and which ones can be incorporated realistically into your schedule. Your personal fitness formula should consist of activities providing results for all three areas of importance: cardiovascular, flexibility, and muscle.

Listed are some samples of exercises and sports and their benefits. I've selected these activities for their practicality for a working woman's schedule. There are many that are not mentioned, such as cross-country skiing, backpacking, and scuba diving, because they involve too much planning and would be virtually impossible to do on a weekly basis.

Benefits of Some Common Exercises

Activity:	Cardio-Vascular	Muscle System	Flexibility
Handball	X	X	
Racquetball	X	X	
Tennis	X	X	
Volleyball	X		
Jogging	X	X	
Racewalking	X		
Walking	X		
Jumping Rope	X		
Cycling (stationary or regular)	X		
Aerobic Dance	X	X	
Ballet		X	X
Karate		X	X
Isometrics		X	
Swimming	X		
Stretching Exercises			X
Jumping Jacks		X	
Nautilus Program		X	
The Office Exercises	X	X	X

To keep things very simple, you should plan on working out for a minimum of thirty minutes, three times a week. Select and combine your activities so that you cover all three benefits. Depending upon the activities you select, you may need two or three activities to do this.

For example, if you enjoy racquetball, you are getting a good cardiovascular workout. You are also benefiting your muscle system. But you are not getting the best exercise for flexibility. So to "round-out" your program, select an activity that offers flexibility, such as stretching exercises. See Sample Fitness Plan #1.

Or suppose you want to do all your exercising at home or in the office. You can jump rope and walk stairs for cardiovascular fitness, and do stretching exercises for flexibility and jumping jacks for muscle strength. See Sample Fitness Plan #2

Sample Fitness Plans

	Cardiovascular	+	Flexibility	+	Muscle Strength	= Executive Fitness
Plan #1	Racquetball	+	Stretching	+	Racquetball	= Fitness
Plan #2	Jump rope	+	Stretching	+	Isometrics	= Fitness

Any number of activity combinations will give you a plan that works well for you. It's best to establish a pattern that is simple and easy to follow. But if you like variety, always keep in mind the three benefits you are after.

When Time is at a Premium

Let's face it. Your heart may be in the right place, but there are going to be days, sometimes even weeks, when you really can't put aside the time to go to your health club, dance class, or even the park to jog. You know you should get some form of exercise every other day—so what do you do? Here are some tips on how to get some exercise during the workday:

In the Company
It is a sign of the times that many of the country's top corporations are developing fitness programs for their employees. You can be sure that despite the seemingly altruistic spirit in which these programs are offered, there is a profit motive involved. Top management is realizing that health and fitness can reap bottom line rewards through more work, less absenteeism, and higher morale.

If your company has joined in the corporate fitness pursuit, you are fortunate and you should definitely take advantage of their programs. It is not unusual for business to be discussed among employees as they work out in the gym. In fact, participation in these programs can lead to higher visibility and strong corporate allies.

But what if your company doesn't offer any type of fitness program? There are a number of options that you can pursue until your company catches up with the

Extra
Edge

trend. And, if you are an action person, perhaps you can use some of the suggestions I offer later to help your company move forward in this area.

If you have your own office, you can exercise there. See the "Executive Office Exercises." Get to the office early and shut the door. Or exercise during your lunch time. If you are going out directly from work, do them in your office after work.

Executive Exercises: An Alternative Plan

The following non-structured exercises can be done at work and to any schedule. They are not meant to replace the other exercises, but to supplement them or be done when time is at a premium:

Exercise #1: Stand straight and reach for the sky as high as you can. Bend over and touch your toes. Stand straight again. With your hands on your waist, twist to the right and then to the left. Do a slight knee bend. Try this 10 times.

Exercise #2: Tighten up each muscle group for a few seconds. Then release. Repeat ten times. The groups to exercise are thighs, buttocks, shoulders, back, stomach.

Exercise #3: Using chair to balance yourself, slowly raise left leg as high as you can in front of you, hold for a few seconds, then lower. Then raise leg to the side slowly, hold, and lower. Finally raise leg to the back, hold, lower. Alternate legs five times.

Exercise #4: Do twenty jumping jacks.

Exercise #5: Standing about a foot from the wall, place your hands against the wall at shoulder height. Press against the wall as hard as you can. Count to six, then relax. Repeat five times.

Exercise #6: Instead of taking the elevator, try walking the stairs at least twice a day. You'll probably be completely alone—hardly anyone even remembers that companies have stairs anymore.

Exercise #7: If you live within a mile of the office and the weather is pleasant, try walking to and from the office several days a week. Or if you're in a hurry in the morning, take public transportation to work and walk home. You can also take a walk after lunch, perhaps with a colleague. You really do need a break from the office and you'll be amazed at how refreshed and revitalized you feel after a good brisk walk.

Bringing Fitness to Your Company

If you don't want to do the exercises in your office, look around the company for an empty room. There's nearly always some room that's never used. You may also find that there are other people in the company who want to exercise. Talk with your personnel office. Point out that some of the top companies in the country have acknowledged the importance of fitness and are profiting from it. You may be able to get an exercise room set aside with company-funded equipment.

Or form a company exercise group, have a room set aside solely for this purpose, and hire an instructor to lead an exercise period during lunch. Many health clubs and exercise salons can provide this service—offering a variety of instructors from aerobics to dance instructors. And if you're as savvy as I think you are, you may get the company to pay for it.

As your company sees the rewards of physically fit employees, you can promote other fitness ideas. Perhaps there is a gym or health club in the company's locale. If so, your company could offer subsidized memberships for its employees. I do recommend that you try to get your company involved in physical fitness programs. In that way, when you take a longer lunch break a couple of times a week to exercise or you want to leave a little earlier once a week to get to the club, you don't risk a disapproving boss. It will definitely make your exercise plan much more enjoyable and easier to follow when you have the company's encouragement.

Calorie Training

As you are probably aware, sports and exercise are good ways to regulate your net calorie usage on a daily basis. Exercise can also be used in conjunction with dieting to lose inches and weight. Although you should see a doctor before beginning any diet, you can start now to "burn off" some calories with exercise. Burning off calories won't get you slim in a hurry, but you can lose weight and inches safely and sensibly. I don't know about you, but I find it more pleasant to burn off calories then to eliminate my favorite foods.

Extra
Edge

Calorie Training Chart:

Activity	To burn about 300 calories:
Running	30 minutes
Walking	60 minutes
Swimming	36 minutes
Ballet	60 minutes
Jumping rope	18 minutes
Karate	30 minutes
Handball	30 minutes
Tennis (*singles*)	30 minutes
Bicycling (*fast*)	25 minutes

What The Executive Woman Should Look For In A Health Club

True to the American entrepreneurial spirit, once the fitness craze began, health clubs of all varieties and sizes proliferated. Many offer a number of services and a competent staff, while others have few services and are poorly staffed. Before you plunk down your hard-earned dollars, do a little research so that you make sure you are getting your money's worth.

Check out the complete facility—don't join on the promise of a new facility or additional services. Assume that you will get what you see. Make sure that you can attend at your convenience. Many clubs require court reservations for activities such as tennis or squash to ensure available court time. This is standard—but you should be allowed to use the rest of the facilities at any time.

- Ask about the staff—what are their backgrounds? Do they have someone with a degree in physical education or exercise physiology?

- Does the equipment look new or well-cared for? Are the pool and the shower areas clean?

- Is someone available to supervise your program—particularly on the weight machines? Or coach in various sports?

- Does your membership fee cover all services or are there extra costs, and are the charges reasonable?

Walking Tall, Walking Proud—The "Executive Walk"

Now that you are getting your body into shape, what better way to show it off than with the "Executive Walk." Good posture not only serves your body well, but creates a stronger, more dynamic image. If you walk with a shuffle and a slump, you are going to look tired, lazy, or bored—hardly the picture of a woman on the rise! You want to look like you're making fast tracks (even if you're only going to the coffee machine).

If you have a full-length mirror, watch yourself as you walk toward it. Is your head erect? Are your shoulders square, your back straight? Do you take strong, confident strides? Do you move forward without swinging your hips? If you do all of the above, you have a good business walk. If not, practice and change it. Below is a description of the most authoritative, professional walk for a woman.

Your arms should hang freely by your sides, not crossed tightly in front of your chest, (something many women subconsciously do), or shoved into your pockets. Your shoulders should be square, not hunched over or rounded. Your head should be held high and your eyes should be looking straight ahead. Tuck your chin in.

As you move, your derrière and your stomach should be gently held in place. Your hips should move forward, instead of side to side. And your arms should swing freely at your side. If you are carrying papers, hold them at your side rather than clutching them to your chest. Schoolgirls carry their papers this way; professional women don't. You want your walk (like everything you do) to reflect confidence, determination, and credibility. Remember, the way you walk can move you "forward" in more ways than one!

Nutrition

This section doesn't attempt to cover all the ramifications of proper nutrition—it's much too broad a topic. But I do want to pass on some advice on eating properly on an executive schedule. At times it may seem like an impossible task—but there are ways to eat just a bit better with a little thought.

The goal of executive nutrition, in addition to the usual benefits of good health, is the achievement of high energy levels. You see, like exercise, what you eat can have a profound effect on how you feel. And a high energy level is a valuable asset in the race to the top of the corporate ladder!

Extra
Edge

The first deadly eating opportunity for the working woman comes in the morning. Too often, she grabs a cup of coffee and heads for the office, where she gets her second cup, or third, or fourth! And if she is like many executives today, she'll have a donut or some other sugary tidbit to keep her energy up until lunch.

I'm not going to tell you that breakfast is the most important meal of the day. (It is, and we've all heard that by now). And I'm not going to prescribe a hearty nutritious breakfast. (Surprise!) Because if you are eating a well-balanced breakfast, you're better than I am and may not need any help on nutrition. But if you don't have the time to prepare eggs, fruit, toast, and juice, I recommend a "Power Drink" as an alternative to coffee on the run. It's quick, tasty, and surprisingly nutritious.

Executive Power Drink Recipes

Using a Blender:

Power Drink #1
Combine 1 cup skim milk, a small banana, 1 tablespoon peanut butter. Blend well.

Power Drink #2
Combine 1 cup skim milk, 2 tablespoons of protein powder and 1 tablespoon of coffee or vanilla syrup. Blend well.

Power Drink #3
Combine 1 cup skim milk, ½–1 cup fresh strawberries, 1 tablespoon Brewer's yeast and 1 teaspoon brown sugar. Blend well.

Lunch

The standard working woman's lunch usually falls into one of two categories: eating on the run or enjoying a leisurely big lunch. Both can be nutritional disasters. The popular chain hamburgers are loaded with astronomical numbers of calories and few nutrients, while the good restaurants offer heavy meals and sauces that can make you drowsy and decrease your concentration for the rest of the day.

Let's take a look at a few fast foods and what you get*:

Product	Calories	Protein	Carbo-hydrates	Fat
McDonald's Big Mac	541	26	39	31
Burger King Whopper	606	29	51	32
Burger Chef Hamburger	258	11	24	13
Pizza Hut Thin & Crispy 10 inch Cheese Pizza	900	50	108	30
McDonald's Filet O'Fish	402	15	34	23
Kentucky Fried Chicken Original Recipe Dinner	830	52	56	46
McDonald's Egg McMuffin	352	18	26	20
Burger King French Fries	214	3	28	10
McDonald's Chocolate Shake	364	11	60	9

By the time you have your Big Mac, french fries and add 100 calories for your non-diet soda, your lunch has earned you 920 calories—almost all of your daily requirement. And you really haven't given your body much in the way of nutrition.

You may prefer having a big meal at lunchtime but this too has drawbacks. Studies have shown that eating a large meal at noon can cause drowsiness, inability to concentrate, and decreased work output. (Haven't we all felt like taking a nap after a big lunch)?

An Alternative Lunch

Look for some of the new restaurants that emphasize salads, fruits, and fresh vegetables. You might have a plate of steamed vegetables with a low-calorie cheese sauce or a pita bread sandwich stuffed with fresh chicken, tomatoes, olives, and other vegetables. An infinite variety of really tantalizing meals can be made from mixing vegetables and chicken, fish, or cheeses. As an added bonus, these foods are much lower in calories.

*Source: Senate Select Committee on Nutrition and Human Needs

If you brown-bag it, make yourself a salad with cheeses and nuts. Add sunflower seeds or sesame seeds and bring a vinaigrette dressing in a separate container so that the salad will not be soggy. Or bring a container of plain yogurt to which you have added your own fresh fruit.

Snacks

I've found that by three o'clock in the afternoon, many working people have begun to hit the company candy machines. They hope that candy will give them a "kick" to get them through the rest of the day. Unfortunately, for many people that effect is temporary and they may wind up with even less energy later. Also, candy is largely a nutritional zero. If you have the urge to snack, why not try something different?

Most health food stores have dried fruits and nuts. Get a variety of these and mix them together for healthy snacking. For example, combine dried apples, banana chips, granola, and peanuts. The combination not only tastes good but can give you a better, sustained energy boost.

If you are thirsty, try fruit juices instead of soda. They will quench your thirst and at the same time give you energy that will last several hours.

Eating Well During a Business Lunch

Conducting business during lunch can be a delicate maneuver at any time. But if you are trying to diet or watch your calories and nutrition, and want to maintain a high energy level when you return to work, it can be difficult. But it's not impossible. The key is to eat a light lunch. Here are some suggestions that can get you through lunchtime without destroying your business or your diet:

- Try substituting a club soda with a twist of lemon for a cocktail.
- Instead of paté, which is high in fat, order broth, fresh fruit, or tomato juice for your appetizer.
- Forego creamy salad dressings; make your own salad dressing with mustard, vinegar, lemon juice, a bit of oil, and fresh pepper.
- Ask for your salad immediately to avoid nibbling on crackers, bread, or dips.
- Select lean meats, chicken, or fish for your entree. Ask for the accompanying sauce on a side dish, so that you can use it in moderation.
- Finish your meal with cheese instead of a sugary dessert and more coffee.

Part III

Success Strategies & Professional Style

Chapter 15

Image and Style Strategies
For The Interview

The first thing you should remember about the interview is that the process is a two-way street. You are there to sell yourself, but equally important, the interviewer is there to sell his or her company. Many people at an interview forget this, become convinced that the interviewer is omnipotent, and are consequently at a disadvantage.

Not only is the interviewer not all-powerful, but he or she may even be at a disadvantage. Even in these highly competitive times, the prospecting company representative must come back to the head office with some qualified potential candidates for the job openings. If the interviewer returns with no candidates, or only a few weak ones, it doesn't look good for him. Believe me, there have been more than a few personnel executives replaced for this very reason.

We will assume that you are familiar with most of the basic guidelines for conducting a successful interview. However, you may have been with the same company for several years and become rusty at interviewing. Perhaps you are a recent college or business school graduate and this is your first corporate interview. In any case, here are some of the basic "rules" for successful interviewing.

Decide Your Direction

The beginning is deceptively simple. Start by asking yourself "what do I want to do now." You would be surprised how many people don't know the answer to this question, or only have some vague notion of where they are going, careerwise.

If you are just out of school, consider which industries interest you. If you have worked for a while, now is the time for some soul-searching about your career. What are you good at, and what really excites you, work-wise? Perhaps a change in direction is indicated. According to the Harvard Business School Career Counseling Center, a little thought at this time can save a lot of headache and heartache later on.

Once you have decided upon a direction, and have arranged interviews with appropriate companies, you should thoroughly familiarize yourself with those companies.

Preparation

Again, this seems very obvious, but a major criticism by executive recruiters is that many prospective employees don't really bother to prepare for an interview with a particular company. Such laxity can have disastrous consequences. Be familiar with the company. Read the Annual Report. Check out the *Wall Street Journal* files at the library to see what has happened at the company recently. Scope out the company through friends and acquaintances to get the "low-down," ideally by contacting someone who already works or has worked there. Find out what kind of interviewing style they have and what interests them in prospective employees.

If you feel that you don't usually come across in a way that you like, practice interviewing. Write a list of the standard questions that companies usually include in their interviews. (By the way, being unprepared for the "stock" questions, which often constitute the bulk of the standard interview, is foolish and unnecessary). Get a tape recorder and use it to record the questions and your answers. Then listen to the tapes. How do you sound? Weak? Uncertain? Inarticulate? What areas need improving? Everyone, (including experienced interviewers) will be surprised at how they sound. Continue practicing with the tape until you like the way you come across.

After you have drilled yourself, ask a close friend or relative who works in a corporation to "interview" you. If your friend is familiar with corporate interviews, he or she will be able to add questions and act as a real interviewer would. Tape these conversations. Again, work on those areas that need improvement.

Another new approach to practice interviewing (which can also be used to develop better communication skills in general) is to use a video camera and conduct a mock interview. This allows you to see your body language in addition to listening to your voice. You can observe how you enter the interview room, how you sit, how you use your hands, whether you move in your seat too much or fidget with your skirt, etc.

Dr. Robert Kent, of the MBA Management Communications Program at the Harvard Business School, thinks this technique should be made an indispensable part of the curriculum for all business schools: "Only by looking at a videotape of ourselves can we really hope to understand how we come across to others. Most people are stunned at what they see the first time, and make dramatic improvements in the way they present themselves after a few sessions with the camera."

These days virtually anyone can afford to rent a video camera/vcr set-up for a short time. (A complete set-up can be rented for as little as $80 for three days, or $150 for a week). Contact a local video store. Many colleges and businesses also have this equipment; consult the audio-visual department concerning its use.

Professional Style and the Hiring Process

Before you are seen, your interviewer will probably have read your resume and become aware of your education and work credentials. Since you have been asked to interview, you can assume that you meet the company's basic requirements. At your first personal interview, which is usually brief, you will be judged on other, less credential-oriented criteria. How you fare here will make all the difference.

As I'm sure you have guessed by now, the most important element standing between you and a job offer at this point is going to be the interviewer's perceptions of your image and style. This is true now more than ever, when many people with excellent credentials are vying for a few management slots.

A Harvard Expert's Advice

According to John Noble, Assistant Director of Harvard University's Office of Career Services, image and personal style are of paramount importance at this point. "We tell our students that in the '80's, more than ever before, how they look and come across is probably more important than anything else. Let's be realistic—there is a large pool of qualified applicants for virtually every job opening."

Noble says that much of the hiring process in America employs a negative, or "pruning" technique. That means that a large applicant pool is steadily whittled down by eliminating applicants until one candidate is left, rather than the right candidate being selected all at once. Negatives in your image or presentation at any step along the way make it easy to be eliminated at that point in the hiring process because the interviewer is looking for reasons to cross people off the list.

Since women are now entering fields that were traditionally male bastions, such as investment banking, consulting, and commercial banking, Noble suggests that it is most important that women look the part. I recommend scouting the industry's and the specific company's image beforehand. Use this knowledge to select an appropriate outfit, accessories, and interviewing style.

You do not have to wear the business "uniform" (you know, the plain navy blazer, A-line skirt, white man-tailored blouse, and scarf). There is more flexibility in appropriate dress for interviewing, and in fact, if you have a savvy interviewer, the uniform could work against you. Following someone else's precise formula for a uniform could convey a lack of confidence and even an inability to think for yourself. However, in general, I do recommend wearing a suit for your interview.

Play it Conservatively

There are unwritten rules for dressing for a professional interview. First and foremost, an interview is a formal business occasion. Consequently, playing things on the conservative side is sound strategy. To show your respect for both the interviewer and the company he/she represents, you should always wear your best business attire.

If the company is part of the financial or the legal world you should dress quite conservatively. Wear a dark suit in winter months, and try a conservative color like tan or gray in warmer weather. The jacket should be a classic style, such as a one- or two-button blazer, or a double-breasted blazer. Your skirt can be any classic design such as A-line, dirndl, or box pleats. Wear a non-frilly silk blouse in a menswear style or with a mandarin or stand-up collar or a soft bow neckline. Most colors, particularly white or iced colors (not pastels), will provide a nice crisp contrast with the suit.

If you are interviewing with a less conservative company, you have more flexibility, but you should still play it safe. The outfit described above would still be appropriate, unless the position for which you are interviewing has a liberal reputation such as in the creative advertising function, art and design depart-ments, or retail buying, when you should display more creativity in your outfit. Here, you could wear a professional-looking dress with a jacket for a more formal look, or a coordinated jacket and skirt with an interesting blouse.

Always wear clothes made of the best materials to interview such as wool or silk. In many managerial positions you are expected to meet with well-educated and upper-income clients—and you must "dress up" to the company's standards. Check *Chapter 7* for further detail.

Accessories and The Interview

Select conservative accessories for your interview. Remember, you will probably never have to dress as conservatively on the job as you do for the interview.

Bring the best briefcase you have. It will subconsciously give the interviewer the impression that you are ready to work immediately. Put a small clutch in it which contains the makeup necessary for a quick touch-up.

Makeup and The Interview

You want to appear cool, professional, and polished. Makeup will help contribute to this image, especially if you are right out of school, if you look young for your age, or if your skin has imperfections. An unmade-up face looks schoolgirl-ish and as a woman, looking too young or naive is a negative. (No one wants to hand over a $100,000,000 investment portfolio to a schoolgirl).

For the interview, follow the makeup plan outlined in *Managerial Makeup*. Use a lighter touch with your makeup color than you would ordinarily use for the office. Remember to apply your makeup in the direct sunlight so that you will see it in the harshest light and can keep the colors soft.

Hair and The Interview

If ever you needed to have a controlled hair style, now is the time. If your hair is long, don't wear it in a loose hair style for the interview. Pin it back with barrettes or in a chignon at the nape of your neck. If you have bangs, make sure that they are well-trimmed and that they do not touch your eyes regardless of how you move your head. Don't try a new hair style on the day of the interview; it may not work out right or you may feel uncomfortable with it. Your hair should look neat, controlled, and unfussy.

Body Language and The Interview

One way that many women can avoid a weak, negative feminine impression is by reducing the amount of hand movement during the interview. John Noble has shown how hand movement can convey strength or softness. Excessive use of the hands is often construed as a negative feminine trait and is an outward manifestation of inner nervousness or lack of confidence. Other signs of nervousness can have a similar effect: picking at nails, twirling a pen, or tapping a finger. In contrast, the controlled use of your hands to emphasize a point appears strong, firm, and "in control."

Noble also suggests that women adopt a more formal posture during the interview. Crossing the legs is certainly acceptable, but be sure you are concentrating on the interview rather than on keeping your skirt covering your knees.

The Big Day— On Into the Foray

The day of your interview has arrived and as any well-prepared businesswoman, I'm assuming you have already selected your complete outfit, and are ready to go. You have thoroughly researched the company and the industry. But these are just the first steps.

Be sure to take another copy of your resume with you just in case the interviewer has misplaced yours. You don't want to spend any of the vital 30 minutes refreshing your interviewer's memory. Plan to arrive 15 or 20 minutes before the interview. Check your outfit, your hair, and your makeup in the restroom. Then you can forget your appearance completely—no wondering whether your slip is hanging or your hair is mussed up. Sit down, relax and watch the people who enter and leave the building. This can give you clues about the everyday workstyle of the company.

Before your interview, check your briefcase to be sure that its contents are secured so that nothing will accidentally tumble out if you need to open it during the interview.

Interview Techniques— Let the Unwary be Warned!

You will probably run across a number of different interviewer techniques during your career, and you should be prepared for all of them.

The Friendly (?) Interview

One of the most common is the "friendly interview," in which the interviewer discusses a variety of topics with you, most of them unrelated to either the job opening or to your qualifications. This approach can work two ways. The correct response may actually be to be friendly and pleasant, and go along with the "chat." But for most professional interview situations, the "friendly interview" may be a well-concealed trap waiting to eliminate you from the running.

The problem is that there is a very good chance that the interviewer is waiting to see if you will "jump in" and take control of the interview—or be ineffectual and continue to let him/her go on wasting valuable time on "chit-chat." Women are often the target of this approach if they are being interviewed by a man. He will want to see how you would deal with other men in the company. Do you follow passively the tone and direction he sets for the interview even if it is going nowhere? Does he get you to talk about your last vacation in Europe, or the office politics at your last company? Don't fall for it. Because if you don't take command, you lose, and that's all there is to it!

Barbara, a first year business school student, almost spent an entire summer unemployed because of this. She interviewed with more than ten companies for a summer job, and was dismayed by her inability to get a single call-back interview. What confused her most of all was that she thought she "had wonderful interviews," and that she had really developed "a great rapport with the interviewers." Many of the interviewers even told her how much they enjoyed speaking with her. What Barbara failed to see was that having a pleasant chat with the interviewer is not what it is all about!

The Pressure Interview

The "pressure interview" or "tough" approach usually starts unexpectedly. You enter the interviewer's office, and out of the blue he starts to "hammer" at you. "What's so good about you?" Or, "Do you really expect me to believe that you singlehandedly restructured the financial analysis procedures at your previous company—come on now!" This frontal attack, in which even your honesty and integrity may be questioned, usually lasts 10 to 15 minutes, and can be devastating to the unwary.

Other varieties of the pressure interview include the "pop" quiz, where you are asked to solve some business or even non-business riddle (some consulting firms love this approach) or where the interviewer gets up, looks out the window, and pretends to completely ignore you. There are even some instances where the interviewer offers you a cigarette if you are a smoker, and waits to see what you do when you realize there are no ashtrays in the room! All of these gambits are designed to unnerve and throw off the interviewee.

The best advice in handling these situations is to stand your guard. Keep a cool head, be aggressive, and firm. Never lose your composure. Always remember, you're doing them a favor by considering their company!

Are There Normal Interviews?

I am not suggesting that you be paranoid and react aggressively in all interview situations. There are still "normal" interviews, where the discussion is relaxed, yet productive dialogue and interchange take place. The best way to decide your approach is to get a sense of the company's self-image beforehand and find out what techniques they use. If they pride themselves on being aggressive and tough, you will have to show them that you can fit right in. But no matter what approach they use, you have one objective—to sell yourself effectively.

And whatever type of interview situation you find yourself in, never let humility get in your way under any circumstance. (No one will sell you unless you do!) And don't waste your time trying to find out about the company or the job, other than to show off your own talents and/or understanding about the requirements of the position. You are there for one reason, to get a job offer. (Let's face it, you should know about the company before the interview. If you don't get the job you don't need to know any more specifics).

Always emphasize the positive in an interview. If you are starting a career or changing careers, think beforehand what your background is and how it will help you to excel at this new job. In fact, what you say is less important than how you handle these potential negatives.

Stock Interview Questions

While you should always prepare for the unexpected, most interviews are quite predictable and consist of so-called stock questions. While I do not recommend "canned" answers to these questions, you really have no excuse for not giving some thought to them prior to your interview. In preparing for your interview you should be ready to answer some of the following questions:

- What are your strengths, weaknesses? (The trick here is to make all of your weaknesses sound like strengths).

- What are your career plans for five years from now? (Have an answer and make sure that your plans are connected to the industry in which you are interviewing).

- What was wrong with your previous employer, or have you ever worked for a boss who was incompetent? (Don't fall into the trap of making disparaging remarks about a former employer).

- Why do you want a job with this company?

- Why did you accept your position with your current employer?

If the interviewer asks you questions that are illegal, and for women this is a definite possibility, don't point out that the question is illegal. I know many people will tell you to speak up and tell the interviewer directly and firmly that there is legislation prohibiting these questions. But, if you do take this stand, it may be a case of "winning the battle and losing the war." You may get the interviewer to back off, but you probably won't get the job. You may be seen as a "troublemaker" and someone that will not "fit" in the organization.

If you are asked any discriminatory questions such as marital status or plans, age, religion, family plans, you should answer deftly and indirectly. For example, "Your family plans are not definite, yet, but whatever they become, they will not affect your performance on the job." Always keep your cool, and smoothly extricate yourself from any such situations.

Executive Recruiters

If you have already started your corporate career, you should develop contacts with one or two "corporate headhunters" even if you are completely satisfied with your current position. In fact, that is the best time to talk with a headhunter. You have much more clout and power when you don't need their immediate service than if you are desperately trying to get a new position. Cultivating some contacts in advance will be invaluable for that time when you want to change jobs.

The best approach is to get the headhunter to call you. There are a number of things that you can do to attract the attention of headhunters—and having a reputation as someone to watch is the best way. The word will get around, and sooner or later you will get a call.

When the time comes that you wish to consider using a headhunter, you should follow a few important rules:

- Never deal with a headhunter whose reputation you have not checked out. There are an incredible number of incompetent or unethical individuals in this field, especially servicing lower managerial positions.

- Never give your resume to a headhunter without specific instructions that it only be circulated to companies you specify in advance. Otherwise, you may be the victim of a "mass mailing" and the word that you are "looking" will get back to your boss sooner than you can imagine.

- If you work for a company that looks unfavorably on its employees even considering other employment (and there are a lot of companies that do) then only accept job interviews if you are seriously considering a change and are prepared to follow through. Don't do it just for the "ego trip" of getting an offer. If the word gets back to your boss, you may have to take a new job a lot sooner than you think!

Chapter 16

Creating Visibility on the Job—
Image & The Promotion Process

You've just been promoted to a bank vice-presidency at Citibank N.A. in New York City. It's an impressive title and you're on your way up the corporate ladder. Or so you think. Unfortunately, there are 500 other vice-presidents also "on the way up" in this major commercial banking institution and the next level has only 100 positions. How do you get to be one of the 100 chosen and not the 400 overlooked?

Perhaps you are a brand manager at Procter & Gamble. Naturally you want to go up the next rung in the marketing hierarchy to a group product-manager spot. You're very good at your job but so are the 60 other brand managers in competition with you for the 15 positions. How do you get singled out for a promotion?

Or maybe you are one of 60 consultants at the Boston Consulting Group. You want to become a vice-president and so do all the other consultants. You are all equally qualified. How do you create the right kind of visibility on the job to ensure your success?

Only a few years ago, woman executives had all the visibility they could handle (though this was a two-edged sword). In fact, a lot of women tried to tone down their visibility by wearing a female version of the male business suit. Well, as I've said before, times have changed. You're not the new kid on the block anymore, and you don't get the automatic recognition that was afforded the pioneer businesswomen. You are now competing with many other highly qualified women, as well as men.

This book is about creating visibility through Total Professional Style. Most of it deals with your physical appearance. In this chapter, we're going to discuss some of the more intangible aspects of a successful business style.

You may find that some of the ideas in this chapter conflict with what you have been told, or even more likely, with what you want to believe about the business world. You may also see them as cynical. They are not. They're realistic. I wish that I could splash a rosy hue on the business world, but it wouldn't be fair to you.

The Real Business of Business

You may think that your job is to get work done at your company. Your title may be "brand manager," "saleswoman," "commercial lending officer," "consultant." But really, all of these jobs are the same. You see, your real job is to please your boss. So, while your title may be brand manager, your job is to make the group product manager look good. Of course, one of the ways you do that is by managing your brand effectively, which in turn reflects well on your boss. But there is much more to it.

The same is true for all other jobs. If you are a saleswoman, you sell X amount, because it makes your sales manager look good. The sales manager encourages you to sell this much because then he* looks good to his boss. And so on up the line because everyone in the corporate world answers to a higher authority.

In this respect, most companies are like the army. There is a "chain of command," and at any particular level each manager is given a substantial "free hand" with

---

The pronoun "he" is used in this chapter only for purposes of simplification, rather than the more cumbersome "he/she."

subordinates. So even if your boss's boss thinks highly of you, if you aren't a winner with your boss, you might as well start looking somewhere else for employment.

If this surprises you, think how often you have seen intelligent and capable people "let go"—people who did their job well and were assets to the company but because they were not liked by their bosses, were fired. Rarely, if ever, will a "higher-up" interfere with the managerial prerogatives of another manager, even a subordinate manager.

The Center of Your Universe, The Boss

Now, a primer in dealing with your boss. The first rule is always, remember who your boss is. He is not a buddy, a protector, a father-figure. Generally he neither likes nor dislikes you. He sees you only as someone who will help make him look good to his boss, or as someone who will not. Knowing this should help you understand your job better.

Don't tell your boss your personal problems. Don't ask for advice on personal matters, or cry on his shoulder, literally or figuratively. He's not interested in the particulars—his only interest is whether your performance is affected, and consequently, his. Many times I have seen an executive's confidences to a boss come back to haunt her. I have even seen a case where the "sympathetic boss" finished his meeting with the confiding employee and then promptly wrote a memo suggesting the employee be moved to a less demanding position due to personal problems. The moral: your boss is not your friend.

Don't ever enter into an affair with your boss. I thought this was a universally understood maxim, but a famous editor of a woman's magazine recently wrote a book in which she encouraged women to have affairs in the office. You may be the one in a million who benefits, but are you so lucky that you can go against such odds?

Keeping on Your Guard

And finally, don't ever let your guard down. And not just with the boss. Don't reveal your personal problems to your peers or your business associates either. They also are not your friends. They are allies when you're a winner and enemies when you're a loser. They may often be competing for the same promotion. And they might use your problems against you.

Jean had six years experience at a top consulting firm. During an after-work drink she made the mistake of confiding to a colleague that she and her husband had been having some problems and that she feared her difficulties might interfere with her work on an important upcoming project. He commiserated with her and made encouraging remarks. Several months later Jean was passed over for a partnership spot. When questioned, her boss informed her that her work had been uniformly excellent. To her astonishment, however, he told her that he felt that a promotion at that time would be too burdensome because she was having marital difficulties.

This doesn't mean to be a stone wall at work, however. Show people innocuous parts of your private life. Look for "safe" topics of conversation to share with others—such as an enthusiasm for racquetball or some other hobby. This will make them feel comfortable around you and will show that you're a reasonable and approachable person (not another "overly aggressive woman" executive). Just remember that "everything you say can, and will be used against you in the 'corporate court' . . ." So don't discuss your latest romance or your problems with the IRS!

Develop a High Profile for Accomplishments

Make sure your boss knows of all your accomplishments. He is not a mind-reader and many of your successes could go unnoticed if you don't post him on them. And remember, you can't count on anyone else singing your praises. Just mention your success briefly and matter-of-factly. Not as if you are "fishing" for praise but rather as if you are posting him on work completed.

Don't be humble. If you are praised for your work, don't react as many women do and downplay your efforts. Leave the false modesty to the Oscar winners. Women often have a difficult time accepting praise or compliments on anything—whether it's on their personal appearance, a promotion they receive, or a job well done. Pay attention the next time a male associate receives "kudos" for his work—see if he attributes his accomplishment to luck, or goes out of his way to spread the glory to others. But don't hold your breath waiting!

Try to come up with new business ideas. (Ones that are realistic and well thought out by you in advance, of course). Propose them to your boss before mentioning them to anyone else. If it's a good idea, let your boss then present it to his boss, giving you some (all if you're really lucky) of the credit. Don't worry if you don't get all the credit. Remember, your boss knows who came up with the idea and will remember that when promotion/raise time rolls around. If he doesn't, make sure you remind him.

How to Look Like You're In Control—Even When You're Not

It's a good practice to keep your boss informed of any major changes in previously agreed-upon projects, or unforeseen circumstances that require a change of plans. This will allow him to evaluate the new situation and be prepared when his boss asks about the change. You would be surprised at how many people fall short in this regard and try to "fight fires" on their own (especially if their mistake caused the problem in the first place). Problems rarely remain quiet for long in companies and not notifying your boss could result in his being caught off-guard by his boss and being made to look foolish.

But that doesn't mean to run to the boss with every little problem that arises, either. Know all of the responsibilities of your position and handle them effectively on your own, within the limits discussed above. Develop an awareness of issues which require his attention and which can be handled on your own. But when a potentially serious problem does come up, try to present some proposed solutions as well, not just the bad news. Your objective is to give the impression that you are always "in control" even when you have a serious problem on your hands. More than a few executives have had their careers "made" when they handled disastrous business problems effectively—even when the original problems were due to their own oversight!

There is, too, such a thing as a Stupid Question!

You've heard it before: "There is no such thing as a stupid question." Don't you believe it. There *are* stupid questions. A stupid question is one that is asked of the wrong person. Think before you ask—"Do I really have to ask my boss this question, or can I ask someone on my level or below?" If you can ask someone else, do it.

This is an especially important problem when you first start at a job and have many questions. It's hard for someone who has been at a job for a long time to remember what it was like when they started. Perfectly reasonable questions may seem "stupid," and the first few months at a job are critical to building a solid foundation for your image, especially with your boss. You are going to find that there are enough questions that only your boss can answer.

Continually asking questions that someone else can answer will not only dilute the amount of useful time you have with him or her, but could give you an image of ineffectiveness. For instance, if you want to see all the previous work on a particular business matter, ask your secretary, who probably has it all neatly filed away. Or ask one of your co-workers. If you must ask the boss, keep a list of your questions and try to go over them all at once.

Seeking Out Winners

Make new contacts, and work at keeping them. Go to lunch or out for a drink on a regular basis with these contacts. You will keep up with what's going on in your company and the industry. (And I'm not referring to the latest office romance). Perhaps you will pick up news about a competitor's new product or an impending industry regulation. Passing this on to your boss can help him perform better.

Learn who the "comers" are at the company and seek them out informally. These people are successful for some reason, and by associating with them you may gain valuable insights into what "works" and what doesn't at your firm.

Make it a special point to develop strong contacts with those people whose work can affect yours. For instance, if you are a marketing manager, cultivate contacts in packaging, R&D, production, sales, etc. When you need a special favor, such as a change in timing on a sales effort behind a new promotion (even though the deadline for such changes has passed), or a rush job on a layout (that you want done in half the usual time), your contacts will prove invaluable. Since they know and like you, they will be willing to put you ahead of others and give your project the extra effort needed to save the day.

When you learn interesting information or have a new piece of data that could be of interest to someone else in your company, drop a brief note or go to see them personally. Tell them you thought of them or their project when you came across the information and that perhaps they could use it. Chances are they'll remember this and return the favor sometime. Or you can subtly ask them to return it when you need help.

Look upon meetings (especially interdepartmental ones), as an opportunity to make contacts and create visibility. Not as the time-wasters they often are. Enter into discussions, slowly at first, until you are acquainted with the politics of the meetings. Always try to say at least one important thing per meeting. Never speak just for the sake of speaking—build a reputation for intelligent suggestions and ideas.

Extra
Edge

A Working Lunch

Although the food in the company cafeteria may be atrocious (or you feel that lunch is a waste of valuable work time), make it a point to eat in the cafeteria at least several times a week. Look upon it as a time to develop new contacts and improve your visibility. Don't get stuck in a rut of eating with the same people; schedule lunch with those outside of your office clique. You'll be amazed at how a few lunches can pay off.

Attend special conferences or trade meetings. We all know that they can be terrible time-wasters in terms of what you actually learn, and many of them are just thinly disguised social occasions. But look at it from another perspective. You may make interesting contacts (perhaps even future employers) and you can usually learn one useful bit of information that you can pass on to the boss or someone in your company. Perhaps you can even circulate a memo on the results of the conference when you return—to the surprise of all of those who thought you were there to have fun!

Become The Office Expert

Make a conscious effort to find an area of business in which you can become the office expert. This does not mean that you have to know everything about the subject. All it means is that you know more than anyone else or have a comprehensive file on the subject. Take the case of Marcy, presently a brand manager for a major consumer packaged goods company.

When she was still a brand assistant, Marcy purposefully set out to become the office "expert" on couponing for packaged goods. She collected studies, read several books on promotion, and soon developed a reputation as the person to see when considering a coupon promotion. She found herself promoted very quickly to the next level in brand management. Now, as part of her yearly career plans, she develops a new area of expertise, whether it is a knowledge of word processing or a handle on the "slice-of-life" form of commercial advertising. Marcy claims this has resulted in two faster-than-average promotions.

Be A Team Player

If your company has sports teams, check into them. Many companies have intra-office sports competitions or groups who play squash or some other sport. If you are already competent in one of the sports, join into the group. You may find once again that you are making valuable contacts and playing with people in a position to help you in your career. If you are really good, you'll find that a lot of people will hear about you in a positive light. (Remember, being a winner is always good for your image).

If you are not adequate in a sport, don't join immediately. You could look silly, or worse, incompetent in front of your business associates. And that image could then carry over to your professional image. Also, anyone who takes playtime seriously (and believe me many people do), is not going to appreciate playing with a neophyte. As a woman your good intentions could actually backfire with this approach. You see, you never want to seem feeble or incompetent at anything. Or you may find that your image suffers. Instead, select a sport at which you have a good chance of competing, and take lessons. Once you can give your instructor a good game, you are ready to play with your colleagues.

When is a Party NOT a Party? When It's an Office Party

If you attend office parties, act as you would in the office. You are not there to have fun, nor are you there to "let your hair down" after a hard day's work. You are on center stage at an office party, particularly since you are a woman.

Always remember, the office party hijinks will be the main theme of company gossip for weeks. If a man and a woman get a little high and start acting overly friendly with each other, it's unfair, but the woman's image will generally suffer much more than the man's. One mistake here and your career could be over at this company. And don't think for a moment I'm exaggerating!

Observe how the powerful people act and don't call attention to yourself at the party. In fact, this is one of the few times you really want low visibility. Spend only a brief time there. Make sure it is known that you attended, but not much more. Have one drink, possibly two if you are sure you can handle it. Then leave. The longer you stay, the crazier the parties usually get. And you don't want to be grouped with the "wild bunch" that got out of hand.

The Politics of Business

A lot of what we have discussed in this chapter has to do with politicking in the corporate environment. The game of politics can be silly, shallow, ruthless, and conniving; it can also be intriguing, amusing, and fascinating. If you turn a deaf ear to the political aspect of corporate life, you will probably find no logic to a lot of what goes on. But don't take it too seriously either. Instead, look upon it as a game—one with self-preservation as a key tenet and survival of the fittest the ultimate objective. Not only will you better understand your company, but possibly even enjoy participating in the "game."

Extra
Edge

Chapter 17

Corporate Finesse—

The Business of Entertaining

You're interviewing for a new job. You've spent two days talking with people from various departments in the company. And now the vice-president of the division is taking you to lunch. You can breathe easily now, you've been hired. Right? Wrong! You're on your way now to the final test.

Your company is wooing a new account and the division manager has asked you to take the account group to dinner. You smile smugly and realize you're on your way up the ladder. You make the reservations. When you arrive at the restaurant your group is kept waiting for 30 minutes before being seated. You may have just slipped on the corporate ladder.

You're about due for a promotion. And this is a big one, a vice-presidency of a very old, very blue-blood investment bank. The senior partner, whom, up to now, you've only met in business meetings, has invited you to lunch with one of the bank's most valuable customers. You're dazzling—until he asks you to select the wine.

What do these situations have to do with your career success? The simplest answer is—a lot! Throughout this book I've discussed the importance of image to your career. How you look, how you dress, the way you speak and act on the job. But because managerial work often involves socializing (especially at the higher echelons), how you handle yourself in social situations can be vital to your career.

Very often today when a person is being considered for a top-level position, an executive will take the candidate to dinner. This not only provides an opportunity for the executive to get to know the prospective employee better under "relaxed" conditions, but to see how they "perform" in social settings. It's also a prime tactic that headhunters use when scouting for new managerial talent. Poor etiquette can result in the loss of a job opportunity or promotion.

Sounds superficial? Of course it is. On the other hand a company has the right to want its representatives to display appropriate savoir-faire. They, too, are being judged by clients, customers, and peers, and they want their people to be deemed polished and sophisticated.

Take something as simple as selecting a wine. A client can't help feeling more respect for the company representative who knows and enjoys good wines, or who can oversee lunch or dinner at an elegant restaurant with style. After all, why should your guest feel you can handle a business matter successfully if you can't orchestrate a dinner smoothly?

For these reasons it is important that as a professional woman you comport yourself with confidence throughout your entire business day. In every situation. This means you should feel at ease in restaurants and in social business situations.

Entertaining for Business

The key times for business entertaining are traditionally lunch, dinner, or drinks. (Breakfast is usually so limited in time that it is only useful for short, strictly business meetings). You really have to experience each to decide what works best for you.

Drinks tend to be almost totally social. Lunch is generally the time to have a somewhat relaxed discussion, with a fair amount of business talk. Dinner usually comes with an implied understanding that there will be a generous amount of socializing but a limited amount of "hard" business discussion.

Discussing business over drinks can be hazardous, and may depend upon your ability to handle liquor. If you can't handle several drinks and retain your business acumen (and most people can't), skip business talk and keep things completely social. Or avoid it all together. I have seen too many sharp, professional people become boring, slow-witted, and embarrassing after several drinks. It's no small task to regain the respect of your companions after such a display, and this is especially true for women. (Another double standard at work!) And don't expect people to excuse this type of lapse as "after-hours letting go." Business is business, whenever and wherever it takes place.

The Importance of Planning

Let's assume that you have decided to entertain a client. The first step to successful entertaining is planning. If you leave the entertaining to spontaneity, chances are it will fail. There are just too many things that can go wrong. Map out every step beforehand.

What's the purpose of your entertaining? Is it to conduct some business, or is it strictly social? If you have a business discussion in mind, you want a setting that provides reasonable privacy for your discussions. If it is social, do you want to impress your guest with a famous, classic restaurant, or should you use your own "special" restaurant that provides incomparable food and a relaxing experience?

Don't make the mistake of burdening your guest with the responsibility of selecting a restaurant. This puts them in a potentially uncomfortable situation—they don't know the size of your budget, or they may not be familiar with the restaurants in your area. Instead, once you have decided on your objective, select two or three restaurants (with different cuisines) that serve your purposes well. Then give your guest a brief description of each to see if they have a preference.

An important "don't" is using entertaining as a chance to explore new restaurants—you could lose credibility (and even your client) if the restaurant is a disaster. I recommend cultivating several restaurants in which you entertain clients. This way you know what to expect, and if you are a familiar face at the establishment you are guaranteed better service. This also helps if you need a special favor or consideration during your meal. And let's face it, it will certainly enhance your image in your guest's eyes if you are accorded respect and personal attention by the maitre d' and the waiters.

Always Make Reservations!

Nothing can get your meal off to a worse start than having to sit around and wait for a table. And it says something about your ability to anticipate potential problems if you can't anticipate the possibility of a crowded restaurant. Don't take chances even if you know the maitre d'—your business entertaining is as important, perhaps even more important, than an in-office meeting.

When you make the reservation, give the restaurant specific details. Your name, your guest's name, and your company. If your company drops a lot of money at that restaurant, it will be reflected in your treatment. But even if it doesn't, the fact that you are a businesswoman will give you clout and gain you preferential treatment. After all, you can recommend the restaurant to other people in your company.

Tell the restaurant when you would like to leave, if you are pressed for time. If you want a leisurely lunch, let the maitre d' know when you arrive so that the waiter will not bother trying to rush you through your meal. If you have a favorite waiter or area of the restaurant, request that location. Check the restaurant's credit policy beforehand. Which credit cards do they take? Not all restaurants take credit cards, or they may not take the ones you use.

To avoid awkward moments at check time, you can discreetly give your credit card to the maitre d' or the waiter when you arrive. You can get your receipt and card at the end of the meal, or better yet, make arrangements for a fixed-percentage tip and sign the credit card invoice beforehand. You can then just get up and depart when you are finished, leaving the impression that you are special and have an "account" at the restaurant. This also works especially well when you are entertaining men who may be embarrassed to have a woman pay the bill and who feel compelled to make some effort to pick up the check themselves. (Yes, there are still some businessmen like that, especially the older ones!)

If the restaurant has a policy of giving a woman a menu without the prices (it's rare these days, but it does still happen), let the waiter or the maitre d' know ahead of time that you are the host. This is one of those instances in which being familiar with the restaurant beforehand can prevent embarrassing moments.

Social Rituals

Like so many things in the corporate world, business entertaining is a ritual. No, the rules aren't spelled out anywhere, but they exist. Consider lunch, for example. Generally there are two types of business lunches. There's the social lunch that is called a business lunch so it can be tax-deductible, and the real business lunch. The purpose of the first (an American business tradition that has kept thousands of restaurants financially solvent), is to have lunch with someone with whom you do business. The objective is simply to make or maintain a contact that is of value to you. No real business need be discussed—in fact it may be counterproductive to do so. The "real" business lunch, on the other hand, contains both elements of socializing and doing business, and is more complicated.

In the case of the real business lunch, the first thing to remember is not to begin talking business as soon as you are seated. This is especially important for women, who are often more accustomed to being entertained than to entertaining, and who may be reluctant to spend time on "small talk," feeling instead a compulsion to "get the job done."

You must understand that business entertaining is a well established, previously all-male, "social ritual." The ritual begins by "breaking the ice," even when it's with someone you already know. If you are a man you would probably be discussing sports or some other "macho" endeavor. Unless this comes naturally, don't fake it. (Nothing is more ridiculous than a businesswoman, or anyone for that matter, trying to "rap" about defensive football plays with a business client when she abhors the game). Instead, discuss subjects of mutual interest. If you have no idea what your guest's interests are, explore various topics until you hit on something. If you are having drinks first, use this time for this type of interaction. Only later, after you have ordered the meal, do you steer the conversation to business.

When the talk finally does turn to business, have some outline in your mind for the rest of the discussion. Don't fall into the trap of sloppy thinking just because the atmosphere is non-business. Your plans should be presented in a clear, direct, and logical manner. After you have discussed the intended topics with your guest, reiterate what you feel is the outcome of the meeting. Make sure that you both agree on the next step in your plans. Once this has been done, drop the business talk and finish your meal on a social note.

If you haven't been able to get the conversation to the business discussion by dessert time, or if every time you bring up business you are side-tracked, forget it. Your guest probably expected a social lunch and any further effort will be unrewarding. Instead, tell them that you have some ideas or plans that you think will be of interest, and suggest a time and place to get together later. An in-office meeting is probably the best bet.

Tipping

Knowing what and when to tip is essential to your style. Overtipping or undertipping can give your host a negative impression of you. I know quite a few people who believe that they can assess a person's character by the way he or she tips. If you overtip, you may appear to be careless with money or trying very hard to impress your host. If you undertip, you may appear to be ignorant or cheap.

It is very important for women to become savvy about tipping. For years many restaurants have given women less than the best service or table, primarily because of a rather universal, although erroneous, impression that women are terrible tippers. You should never put up with this treatment—demand good service and good tables, and tip accordingly.

One of the biggest mistakes people make is tipping when they receive poor service. You are not obligated to tip and if you feel that the person did not perform the service to your satisfaction, assert yourself and reduce the tip accordingly. If you choose not to tip at all because of the poor service, tell the maitre d' or the captain. This will preclude an impression that you are merely cheap. If, on the other hand you were provided with special service or attention, you should show your appreciation and tip more than the standard.

How Much Should You Spend?

Before you begin your business entertaining, check out your company's "norms" and stay within them. Find out from your co-workers what restaurants they frequent. That will give you an idea of restaurants that are appropriate for conducting business, and how much the company tacitly expects you to spend. (This is another one of those things you just don't come out and ask your boss about. You must find it out some other way).

More often than not, you will be surprised at how much your company approves and even expects, to be spent on entertaining—$30, $50, or even $70 per person is not unusual in some circumstances. There are several reasons for this. The first is that having the company pick up the tab is one of the few remaining, untarnished perks that separates the white collar from the blue collar in these days of corporate "belt-tightening." Also, business entertaining is a reflection on the company, and doing it right is important to its long-term image. And, after all, Uncle Sam picks up the tab for half of the cost since it's a deductible business expense!

Extra
Edge

A Guide to Tipping

The following are guidelines for tipping:

Maitre d':	Generally not tipped unless he/she provides you with a special service.
Captain:	Oversees your waiters and should receive a 5–10 percent separate tip.
Waiter:	15–20 percent of the bill before tax.
Wine Steward:	About 10 percent of the wine bill before tax at time of service.
Bartender:	If your bar bill is separate, tip the server 15 percent
Cloakroom Attendant:	Tip at least 50 cents per coat.*
Ladies' room Attendant:	25 to 75 cents if she provided service.*

Being Reimbursed

If you have a credit card, (and it is unprofessional not to have one), try to use that most of the time. That will give you an automatic receipt for most of your large expenses, and will eliminate the hassles of getting cash advances from the company or using your own cash. Simply fill out an expense report with the receipt, and get reimbursed.

Many companies will not request receipts for items such as taxis, parking, and tolls. But keep track of all of these small expenses since they do add up quickly. Don't delude yourself into thinking that the company will appreciate your subsidy of their business if you absorb these small, non-receipted expenses yourself. I know of one young businesswoman who dreaded long business trips because she always lost $75 or so on each one. On her return, she would only seek reimbursement for those expenses for which she had receipts. This was nonsense, of course.

*A word about one of my pet peeves. There is a common practice among coat and ladies' room attendants to leave a dish in full view filled only with dollar bills. Often one bill is taped or glued down. This prompts many people to leave a dollar because they are afraid they will look cheap if they are the only ones leaving coins. Don't be maneuvered by this ploy into leaving more than you feel is appropriate.

If you entertain or travel frequently, and want to avoid the headache of reconciling your own personal credit card statements, look into using a company credit card for all of your business entertaining. These cards can be issued with your name and the company name, and the bill goes directly to the accounting office.

Other Aspects of Executive Etiquette—Dining Savoir-Faire

When entertaining for business, you want to strengthen your image as a sophisticated businesswoman—one who is at ease with any situation. One way that you can accomplish this is by subtly demonstrating your knowledge of food and wine. If it's a client you're entertaining, he or she will be impressed if you seem to be at ease with a gourmet menu or an extensive wine list. On the other hand, you may appear somewhat naive to your guest if you have to ask the waiter to describe fairly well-known dishes or fumble with the wine selection.

International Repasts

Generally speaking, when you are entertaining for dinner in a sophisticated fashion, you will most likely be eating at an American, French, Italian, or Oriental restaurant. These appear to be the most popular choices among business people for entertaining. I've listed some dishes with which you should be familiar.

A Guide to Dining Out

French

Coquilles Saint-Jacques	scallops in wine sauce
Caneton a' l'orange	duckling with orange sauce
Poulet a' l'estragon	chicken with tarragon sauce
Coq au Vin Rouge	chicken in red wine sauce
Boeuf Bourguinon	beef stew cooked in a red wine (Burgundy) sauce
Ratatouille	eggplant, zucchini, pepper, and tomato ragout
Vichyssoise	a chilled potato and leek soup
Bouillabaisse	fish and shellfish soup

A Guide to Dining Out (Continued)

Steak Tartare	raw ground beef of top quality, garnished with seasonings
Poulet Marengo	chicken casserole with tomatoes and mushrooms

Italian

Cannelloni	rolls of pasta with various fillings
Osso Buco	braised veal shanks
Spaghetti alla Carbonara	spaghetti with eggs, bacon, and cheese
Pasta e Fagioli	a hearty bean and pasta soup
Spaghetti with Amatriciana Sauce	spaghetti with pork, pepper and tomato sauce
Pasta con pesto	pasta with basil, pine nut, and cheese sauce
Fettucine Alla Panna	flat noodles in a butter, cream and cheese sauce
Veal Scallopine alla Marsala	veal in Marsala wine sauce
Chicken Florentine	breast of chicken on bed of spinach

Oriental

Tempura	seafood and vegetables dipped in batter and deep fried
Sukiyaki	vegetables and beef broiled in a soy sauce mixture

A Guide to Dining Out (Continued)

Teriyaki	marinated beef glazed with soy, garlic, and ginger sauce and broiled
Mo-Shu Pork	a pork and oriental vegetables mixture wrapped in thin pancakes
Sushi	raw fish

Other

Beef Stroganov (Russia)	beef with mushrooms in sour cream sauce
Chicken Kiev (Russia)	deep fried chicken breast with butter and herbs
Borscht	Russian beet soup
Moussaka (Greece)	eggplant and lamb casserole
Shish Kabob (Turkey)	generally, skewered lamb and vegetables
Welsh Rabbit/Rarebit (England)	melted cheese with beer served on toast
Carbonnades a' la Flamande (Belgium)	beef and onions braised in beer
Chicken Divan	poached chicken on broccoli with Hollandaise sauce
Sweetbreads	the thymus of a young animal (usually a calf)

Restaurant terms with which you should be familiar:

table d'hote	complete meal of several courses at a fixed price.
a la carte	each item on the menu is priced separately.

Extra
Edge

Wine—The Perfect Dinner Accompaniment

Since drinking wine is still a relatively new custom in America, many people are intimidated by the prospect of ordering it. The idea becomes even more nerve-wracking when you have to select a wine for others, particularly business associates whom you are trying to impress. But as wine becomes increasingly popular and often replaces the traditional hard drinks, you may find yourself in the unenviable (to many people) position of selecting the dinner wine for your table.

There is a lot of pretense and snobbery associated with wine. And many people feel that they must "put on airs" to impress others with their knowledge. If that's your intent, there are many books on the subject. I'm just going to discuss some rudimentary guidelines for selecting a wine that will be a pleasant accompaniment to your dinner and please your guests.

There are three things that you should know about wine—where it comes from, how much it will cost, and what it will taste like. When presented with a wine list, you cannot always opt for the most expensive wine and assume that you have made a good choice. In fact, you are probably displaying your ignorance on the subject rather than impressing anyone. The most expensive wines are not always the best for a number of reasons—and they may be completely inappropriate for your meal. And you should not assume that any French wine will be good. Many are overpriced, thus making many American wines much better values.

Wine Tasting

There is a great deal of hoopla and showmanship associated with the tasting of wine. After you have ordered, the wine steward will bring the unopened bottle to you and show you the label. Then the wine is decanted or opened and the steward usually places the cork on the table. Although many people do not realize it, the cork can tell you a great deal about the wine.

- Inspect the cork. If it is dry and crumbly, air has gotten into the wine and it will be bad. If it smells vinegary, the wine will not be good either.

- If the cork passes muster, the steward will then pour a small amount of wine into your glass for your approval. You should hold the glass up to the light to check the color—it should be clear and brilliant, indicating a fine, healthy wine.

- Next you smell the wine. Agitate the wine in the glass first to release the maximum quantity of esters. A wine expert can tell whether the wine is clean or unclean, young, mature, or old; and even its origin. If you are a novice you will probably only notice if the wine is bad.

- Finally, the taste. Take a small amount of wine into your mouth and gently agitate it again by sucking in air. This should release maximum taste. Then swirl the wine around in your mouth to get the full taste. Do this final step only if you are very skilled because it can look sloppy. Otherwise, just take a small amount of wine in your mouth and gently swirl it, then swallow.

The idea is to do these steps naturally and subtly, without seeming pretentious. If you experiment with wines at home and among friends, you will begin to know which tastes and types of wines you prefer.

There are some people who occasionally feel compelled to send back a bottle of wine, claiming that the taste is slightly off, to show their guests that they are true connoisseurs. This tactic loses more respect than it gains, unless the wine really is bad. Generally speaking, it is extremely rare that a bottle of wine should be returned, provided it is the one that you ordered. If a bottle of wine is bad, you will know it immediately. And your steward will, too.

Matching Wine and Food

You should be aware of the general rule for ordering wine with your meal. Most people tend to feel that a hearty red wine (bordeaux or burgundy) is an appropriate complement to a red meat meal. While a white wine is best with fish or seafood. Again, this is just a general rule.

Essentially, dry white wines are well-suited to all fish and seafood, and to pork and delicate dishes such as sweetbreads. Sweet white wines are best with desserts. Red wines complement pates, beef, lamb, mutton, game and pasta dishes. Chicken, turkey and other poultry, and veal are complemented by either red or white wines except when served in a cream sauce, which calls for a dry white wine. A dry champagne is the one drink that complements all foods and is appropriate at any time.

During the course of a single meal, the traditional rule is to serve white wines before red wines, young wines before old wines, and dry wines before sweet wines. In other word, just as a menu proceeds from light dishes to richer dishes, you proceed from light wines to rich ones. And it is really only common sense. After a fine old burgundy, a light young wine would suffer by comparison.

"A Wine Primer" includes a list of types and terms that are useful to know for business dinners.

A Wine Primer

Red

Beaujolais	Fresh, fruity and dry.
Bordeaux	Soft taste, excellent flavor. *Cabernet Sauvignon* is one of the best.
Burgundy	Full body and flavor. *Pinot Noir*—one of the best. Dry.
Chianti	Round, full flavor. Dry.
Sangria	Spanish fruit punch. Semi-sweet.
Valpolicella	Delicate, soft and smooth. Dry.
Zinfandel	Fruity, delicate. Medium dry.

A light red wine is preferred if only one wine is served for the entire meal. A burgundy, which is much heavier, is usually the choice for the red meat course, if more than one wine is served for the meal.

White

Asti Spumanti	Champagne. Sweet and sparkling.
Chablis	Medium body, crispy. Dry.
Chenin Blanc	Soft and fruity. Medium dry.
Haut Sauternes	Full. Sweet.
Liebfraumilch	Slightly sweet. Medium dry.
Pinot Chardonnay	The best full flavor white burgundy. Dry.
Pouilly-Fuisse	Fruity and crisp. Dry.
Sauterne	Medium body, fruity. Medium sweet.
Soave	Refreshing. Medium dry.
White Bordeaux	Smooth refreshing. Medium dry.

Sauternes and *Barsac* produce the most luscious sweet white dessert wines in the world.

At lunch, dry white wines are served almost exclusively.

Rosé

Mateus	Bubbly soft wine. Medium dry.
Rose d' Anjou	Light body and flavor. Dry.
Tavel Rosé	Pleasant dry taste.

A *rosé* is not considered as fine a wine as either the red or the white. It is often a compromise selection for people who are unsure of which wine is appropriate.

Wine Terminology

Below are some terms with which you should be familiar.

appellation controlee	controlled name of origin. Signifies a French wine of an agreed standard of quality and production from a named area.
chateau bottled	Bordeaux wines bottled on the estate where they are grown.
claret	another name for bordeaux wine.
corse	wine that is full bodied and robust.
cru classe	the wines of Medoc, Graves, St. Emilion and Sauternes which are officially classified as leading growths.
cru exceptionnel	special category of seven bourgeois wines that are ranked immediately below the cru classe.
cru bourgeois	a Medoc wine of good quality but lesser standing than the classified growths.
cuvee	in Burgundy it signifies a wine from the best pressing; in Champagne it indicates a blend of different wines.
demi-sec	half sweet wine
doux	sweet
sec/brut	dry

Extra
Edge

Chapter 18

Business By Day—

Glamour By Night

Many working women today find that they often go out socially after work. And many prefer to go out straight from the office rather than go home to change. In the past, this has presented a problem, since the business uniform that was popular a few years ago was hardly appropriate for an evening on the town. But, as I've said before, times have changed and today you can look professional in the office and glamourous in the evening without changing your entire outfit.

The key word is accessories. By changing your accessories you can completely change the look of the suit or dress that you wore to the office. You really have great flexibility in the outfits that you wear to the office so that you can look both fashionable (in a positive sense) and professional. The materials that the designers are using in today's suits are very different from the heavy, almost stiff kind previously used, and the lines and styles of the clothes are much less rigid. This means, very simply, that the suit you wore to the office today can be worn to that chic little French restaurant tonight.

Before we discuss ways of making your suit work day and night, I want to take exception to the stand that a male consultant on success dressing has taken. According to John Molloy: "The skirted suit is not effective for social occasions. The suit gives you authority and a sense of presence in business. But that's not what most women want on social occasions. They want to be attractive and have fun."

Well, you've done it again, John! First of all, most professional women that I know want to have a "sense of presence" in social occasions as well as in business. I don't see how such presence is mutually exclusive with being attractive and having fun. And, as far as women wanting to be attractive and have fun during social occasions, well, our male co-workers appear to want the same thing!

Now that you know my feelings on the use of the suit, let's discuss some practical ways to glamorize your professional outfits without having to dash home and spend several hours dressing up.

Quick Change Artist

I'm partial to dark suits when planning a day-to-evening schedule, but many colors are appropriate. For simplicity's sake, let's use a black suit (which by the way is always fashionable and has a very strong "authority" image).

When discussing the versatility of a suit, its fabric is an important element. Obviously a heavy or bulky fabric is much more difficult to transform into an evening look. Your best bet is to look for suits in durable but lightweight fabrics such as wool flannels, wool crepes, gabardine, silks, linens, or blends of natural fibers like wool and silk, linen and silk, etc. Basically, you want a fabric that has fluidity or movement.

The illustration shows an example of a professional-looking suit, accented with accessories that work well for the office. Next to it, the same suit is accessorized for evening wear. As you can see, with a few changes you can go out on the town. You are no longer a madwoman racing home from the office, changing, and dashing off to the restaurant or the theatre. And you have also saved yourself the cost of an evening outfit.

Two-Piece Outfit

This is another type of outfit that affords great flexibility when it comes to day-into-evening plans. During the day, the two pieces work as a business-like dress; at night, you have the luxury of changing either piece for a completely different look. Two of the best materials for this type of outfit are silk and wool challis.

Extra
Edge

Day Into Evening

You can create an evening look with a few quick changes right in the office.
Change your blouse to a camisole; and a necklace and dressier earrings; change your stockings.
Carry an evening clutch instead of your regular handbag.

Dresses

Although a dress cannot generally offer as much contrast between day and evening looks, there are ways to make your outfit more festive. If you have a solid color silk dress, you can use small subdued accessories for the day and larger, more eye-catching ones at night. By changing your earrings, adding a fancy belt, and putting on dressier stockings and shoes you are ready for your night out!

Nighttime Makeup

Using the new approach to executive dressing for women, we are able to create an outfit that is appropriate for a restaurant, a movie, the theatre, or cocktails with a few simple changes. The same is true for your makeup. With a little advance planning you can create a nighttime makeup look in a matter of minutes.

As we've already discussed, you should have some items at work for daytime touch-ups. If you occasionally go out at night directly from the office, you should expand your touch-up kit to include everything from face cleansers to nail polish to makeup for an evening on the town. Keep only items such as lipstick, compact, touch-up stick, blusher, and lipliner in your purse since you may need these if you have to leave the office. Leave the rest in your desk.

If you plan to spend the evening out and want to start with a fresh face, use the following guide. If you are just going out briefly after work, you can skip to Step 4.

Put your headband on so that you can clean your face and apply makeup without getting water or makeup in your hair.

1. Cleanse your skin with your regular cleanser.

2. Again, depending upon your skin type, apply toner or moisturizer.

3. If your mascara has smudged underneath the eye area, remove all traces of mascara from the skin with a cotton swab dipped in a non-oily eye makeup remover. This allows you to reapply eye makeup without worrying about oils around the eye area.

4. Reapply foundation with a damp sponge and then your blush. For nighttime, you can use any color you wish, unless it's a business occasion. If it's strictly business, just increase the intensity of your office colors.

Extra
Edge

Nighttime Makeup Tips

1. For All-Over Sparkle!!

For special nights out, try a light brush of iridescent face powder on cheeks and around the eye area.

2. Dramatize Your Eyes!!

Add a frosted or gold-flecked highlighter—such as sunset pink, bronze, or champagne—you can apply it right over your day highlighter. It will give your face a warm, candlelit glow.

If you used brown or grey as your day shadow, add a brighter color over it on the lid such as loden green or even soft blue—the two colors will blend to give just a subtle hint of the new color. Or brush the gold or pink lightly over your entire lid, right over your day colors. Or add a new color in the crease.

With the corner of your eyeshadow brush, run a deep color along the lower lashes. This will "lock in" your eyeliner, and if done correctly can make your eyes appear much larger, and more dramatic.

Extend your eyeliner beyond the corners of your eyes. And then smudge it. Try a different color liner such as a deep blue or deep green or violet.

3. Light Up Your Lips!!

Dab a tiny spot of your gold eyeshadow or pearl gloss in the center of your lips for a pouty look.

Or try highlighting your lower lip with a very pale frosted lipstick placed over your regular, deeper lipstick and blended well.

4. Spice Up Your Skin!!

With the large powder brush, sweep the softest pink or golden beige powder blush you can find across your forehead, around your eyes, at your temples, on your chin, on your throat, at your ear lobes.

Day To Night!

Be more adventurous with your nighttime makeup. I have given you some hints for putting glamour into your looks, and below are some colors to try for more sizzle.

Product	Suggested Night Colors
Foundation	Skintone or several shades lighter for a really dramatic look
Powder	Translucent, skintone, or try iridescent gold or pink
Blush	Rose/plum/mauve/tawny/beige/wine/pink/fuschia
Eyeshadow	Shiny/frosted/gold flecked/opalescent almost any color works at night
Eyeshadow/highlighter	Flat/Frosted/Metallic gold/bronze/yellow/peach/pink/white
Lipliner	Apricot or apple, or whatever matches your evening lipstick
Lipstick	Matte/frosted/or gloss. Any color from palest pink to deepest red
Eyeliner	Navy/slate/deep green/violet/black charcoal/dark brown
Mascara	Black/navy/violet

Some Accessory Tips for Evening Sparkle

These are some tips for adding "pizazz" to your outfit. One word of caution, though. When you are changing your office look, don't merely throw on lots of accessories and think that you now have an evening look. It isn't that simple. If you have a very fancy belt, don't make it compete with an elaborate necklace and eye-catching earrings. Highlight one or two accessories, and that's all.

- Long dangle earrings or intricately designed ones can dress up your look.
- An unusual belt will add glamour to your outfit.
- Try lace or dotted stockings instead of plain ones.
- A higher heel or a strappier shoe will give an evening look.
- Exchange your office handbag for an evening bag.
- An extravagant-looking necklace, which you wouldn't wear to the office, might be just right for the evening look.

Extra
Edge

Chapter 19

Travel in First Class Style

More and more women are traveling for business (running up a total of 28 million business miles last year), and that means extra work to ensure that you keep up your Professional Style. Not only do you want to look good during your flight, but you want to be impressive when you arrive at your destination.

This was an especially difficult situation for women in the past when they were locked into several rigid and distinctly different roles—the executive conducting business in the uniform and the woman socializing in her cocktail dress. As we've discussed before, there is no longer the need to make such a sharp delineation between your office and your social image. Consequently, maintaining a 24-hour-a-day professional image while on business travel is much easier today.

The biggest mistake women make is overpacking. Instead of packing a daily "new outfit," with a little thought and creativity, the traveling businesswoman can reduce the amount of clothes she packs and still present a polished image for each occasion.

It is also true that most people, both men and women, do all the wrong things for their physical well-being during travel—by the time that they arrive at their destination they may look haggard and feel even worse. This is not surprising, especially when you consider that flying means small confining seats, pressurized cabin air, and less-than-exciting meals.

Plan Your Trip

Planning your trip is the most important part of traveling. If you have thought out the business purpose of your trip and whether you want to combine any social/sightseeing times, you can avoid a lot of problems once you arrive at your destination.

Find out about the city that you are going to visit. Ask your travel agent and business associates for a list of restaurants, theatres, museums, and other things of interest. When you arrive, check out the newsstand for local papers and magazines. Many major cities now have their own magazine which gives an in-depth listing of area events and sights. Talk with the hotel manager, ask for his or her recommendations on places to visit while you're in the city. And take the time to get to know the city—don't make it all business. You'll feel much better about your business if you have the time to relax and enjoy your surroundings.

Decide which hotel location would be more convenient for you: in the center of the city, near the outskirts, or in the suburbs. This will ameliorate any problems with parking your car, finding a taxi, or getting caught in the morning traffic rush. If you are attending a convention at the hotel, try to arrive and depart on the off-hours so that you will not spend your time standing in lines to check in and out.

Give yourself time to relax before your business meetings. If at all possible, arrive the night before, have a hearty meal, and get a good rest. You'll wake in the morning refreshed and relaxed for your meetings.

If you can't leave the night before, leave in the morning. But don't go to the office first to try to squeeze in a few hours work. On my first business trip, I had everything planned so that I would not waste a minute. I skipped breakfast, went into the office with all my luggage, worked for an hour, raced to the airport and arrived in an agitated state with fifteen minutes to spare. There I caught up with the three men with whom I was traveling—they had skipped the office and arrived at the airport to enjoy a leisurely breakfast! Needless to say, I never made that mistake again.

Extra
Edge

Diane Shaib, vice president at American Express, has helped develop a series of tips for the successful business trip:

- If your company doesn't have its own corporate travel department or an outside agency, rely on a well-versed travel agent to make your hotel and transportation arrangements.

- Protect your reservation by charging your hotel room to a major charge card. Ask for written confirmation or, if there is not enough time, a confirmation number of your hotel reservation.

- Try to get round-trip seating assignments and boarding passes when you reserve a flight. If you can't get a seat assignment in advance arrive early at the airport for a better seat.

- Ask your agent to send your tickets to you well in advance of your departure, and check them for errors.

- If connecting flights are involved, ask your travel agent to find out gate locations of the connecting flights. Double check all baggage claim tags to make certain they are tagged for correct destinations.

- If you are on a tight schedule, find out about transportation from the airport before departure and make the necessary arrangements.

- Send bulky items or heavy equipment ahead and have your hotel hold the material.

Managing Your Money

Planning your finances is an important aspect of business travel. Make sure that you budget enough cash to cover taxi fares, tips, and incidentals. Put a fair amount of your cash in the form of travelers checks, especially if it is to be a long trip, since they can be replaced immediately if lost or stolen.

Keep your cash expenditures to a minimum. Rely instead upon credit cards. This way you have a permanent record of your expenses (they come with your bill) and you won't risk losing reimbursement from the company upon your return because you forgot about the expenditure.

Bank and travel cards are not only convenient, but often essential to effective and hassle-free traveling. Many companies are reluctant to issue cash advances that are large enough to adequately cover the exigencies of a trip; or they expect you to charge the expenses to your credit cards and be reimbursed upon your return. If that is the way your company handles business travel, you will need special permission to get a large cash advance if you do not have a card, and this is the kind of attention you will want to avoid—it is unprofessional and unwise for a businesswoman not to have credit cards.

You should also be aware that it is usually not possible to rent a car without a major credit card. I know of one young woman who had to resort to the extraordinary step of handing over her paycheck to a car rental agent as security for a car!

Your best bet is to get those credit cards without any particular credit limit, such as the American Express card. Most bank cards have specific limits that cannot be exceeded. After all, do you really want to cope with a cross-country business trip on a $750 bank card credit limit?

Tips on Tipping

Tipping customs vary somewhat throughout the country, usually the higher tips are expected in the larger metropolitan cities. The following should give you an indication of standard tipping practices. If you are ever in doubt as to the appropriate tip, ask the manager of the hotel or the restaurant.

Your Hotel

Have you ever arrived after a long, hectic trip to seek solace in your hotel room only to find that it's small, next to a constantly running elevator, and the view is that of another building? It's happened to most business travelers at least once. But there is no need to grin and bear it.

Decide ahead what type of room you want. Do you like two large beds even if you're alone? Do you want to be on a high floor away from the noise of the traffic or do you prefer to be close to the first floor? Would you like to be located near the hotel pool or sauna? Ask for it ahead of time. If you plan meetings in your room, request a suite where sleeping and living areas are partitioned.

Decide in advance what services and equipment you want at your hotel. Have your travel agent call to check that it has everything you will need. Always bring along your own alarm clock. One of the new palm-sized electronic pocket alarms is especially appropriate, since they are so tiny. In either case, your own alarm can be a life-saver as a back-up to the hotel morning wake-up call, which occasionally doesn't come.

Traveling Tips
"How to Tip"

Porters, Bellhops:	$1 per bag
Taxi Drivers:	10 to 15 percent + 75 cents per bag of luggage
Doorman:	50 cents to $1 if he gets you a taxi in inclement weather.
Hairdresser:	20 percent for the stylist; $1 for person who washes it
Manicurist:	$2 to $4
Room Service:	15 percent

If you receive a special service you may tip anywhere from five to twenty dollars depending upon the difficulty or the degree of extra special service. For instance, if you receive the best table in the restaurant or the hotel concierge has located an outside person to assist you in a business matter, you may tip $20.

If you are staying at the hotel for several days it is best to be generous with tips, especially with those people with whom you will continue to interact. It assures continued good service, which will come in handy when conducting business at the hotel.

Special Hotel Services

Depending on the quality of your hotel you may find some of the following services available. Ask and take advantage of them. It is important for you both personally and for the quality of your work, to allow yourself time to relax and get energized, something that is especially important on a prolonged trip. Some hotels:

- have pools, saunas, or some type of fitness facility. Find out beforehand so that you can bring your bathing suit or other appropriate sportswear.

- have special concierge floors. Room rates are higher, but you'll find more privacy and luxury. There's usually a separate elevator, lounge, services of a concierge, complimentary cocktails, hors d'oeuvres, continental breakfasts, and amenities such as bathrobes and special shampoos.

- offer complete business centers, including secretarial services and equipment, rental office space, telex, reference library, research facilities, and courier services.

- offer shuttle buses or vans to key business areas and sights.

- have special floors for smokers and non-smokers.

Now that you have the details of your trip planned for success, let's discuss how you can arrive looking relaxed, refreshed, and ready for business.

Fresh Facade

The key to stepping off the plane with a polished look is your outfit. Make sure that your outfit is first, non-fussy—straight clean lines and colors as close to monochromatic as possible—and second, wrinkle-free. The less fussy your outfit, the more together your image will be. Look for quality fabrics that are wrinkle-resistant such as knits (of wool, cotton, silk, etc.), wool flannels, wool or rayon challis, gabardine, and ultra-suede.

A good test for determining whether an outfit is wrinkle-resistant is to scrunch the material in your hand for about 30 seconds, then release. If the wrinkles don't brush out easily, you'll have problems.

If you wear a suit, don't keep the jacket on during the flight. Hang it up so that it will look fresh when you leave the plane. (Most planes have small closet areas in the front or rear of each section where jackets can be hung. Use them, instead of laying your jacket out flat on the overhead rack). Opt for dark colors, which will show wrinkles or creases less than lighter colors; they also give a crisp, fresh look. For comfort, especially during a long flight, try classic-looking trousers in a menswear fabric such as flannel. Or consider carrying your outfit on a hanger and changing in the lavatory before you arrive if you are being met at the airport.

Your Business Wardrobe

Key to packing for a business trip is making the most from the least. You want to pack sparingly but at the same time, you need to be able to dress for an early morning appointment, meetings during the day, and socializing at night. You

Extra
Edge

191

Traveling Tips
"Hotel Safety"

While the chances are slim that you will ever have a problem with security or fire in your hotel, it's always best to take precautions. This is especially true in light of a number of well-publicized tragedies involving business hotels in the last few years.

Some valuable safety precautions to keep in mind are:

- Avoid rooms at the end of long corridors. Request a room next to the elevator or midway down the hall. If you arrive late don't hesitate to have a bell-hop escort you to your room.

- Avoid ground-floor accommodations. Make certain that rooms with balconies have sliding doors that lock. Double check the lock on the doors. But do get a lower floor, if possible, so you can jump or be reached by a fire ladder easily.

- Locate the fire exit nearest your room as soon as you check in. Know exactly how many doors there are between your room and the exit. Ask the hotel clerk about fire alarms and make sure the one in your room is working. Or bring your own, small portable travel type fire alarm.

- Don't leave "Please make up this room" signs on your door, since this announces that you are not in. Don't hesitate to use the hotel safe for your valuables, or check valuable equipment at the front desk rather than leave it unattended in your room for long periods.

- Before you go sightseeing or jogging, check with the desk to find out about any high crime areas to be avoided.

should really put a lot of thought into what clothes and accessories you bring. In general, a good rule of thumb is to pack one or two basic outfits and then add a variety of accessories to change the look of the outfits. You also have to take into consideration the climate of your destination.

Traveling Tips

"Sample Wardrobe"

- One two-piece suit in a lightweight, wrinkle-resistant fabric such as gabardine or wool crepe. Dark is preferable since it will show less dirt and wrinkles.

- A two-piece dress in a color and print that compliments the suit.

- A blouse that will mix and match with both the suit and the dress.

- A silk camisole to wear with the suit or the skirt for dressy evenings.

- Two pocketbooks, one sturdy leather for day and a small, dressier clutch for evenings.

- Two pairs of shoes: walking pumps and a dressier style such as slingbacks.

- Inexpensive (replaceable) earrings and necklaces. Select several distinctly different earrings for day and larger earrings for night.

- At least five or six pair of stockings. Bring some stylish dark patterned stockings for evenings and several different colors for day.

- Two or three belts. One practical belt and perhaps a sash to give a different look.

- Sweater and a pair of pants for non-business walking tours.

Travel Makeup

In the morning of your flight, apply foundation to your clean face. Apply your lipliner and your lipstick. Add a touch of mascara. That should be all you use for the flight. The foundation and the lipstick (if you're using the right kind) should help keep your skin and lips from drying out during travel.

About an hour before your arrival, use the ladies' room to finish your makeup. Remove your lipstick. Add the appropriate blush for your skin, whether it is creme or powder. Brush on a light finish of pressed compact powder to freshen up your skin. Brush on your eyeshadow. Line your lips and fill in with lipstick. Now you look refreshed and rested.

I generally do not recommend applying mascara or eyeliner during flight because of the danger to your eyes. Turbulence or an air pocket could cause you to injure your eye. Avoid potential hazards—you can always add more makeup once you are in the airport.

Special Skincare

If you are going on an overnight flight, I would recommend cleansing and moisturizing your face before you board and not using any makeup. In the morning, wash your face with your own soap or cleanser. Do not use airline soap—it's usually either too drying or scented, both of which are bad for your skin.

Since most of the time on an overnight flight you'll be traveling alone to your business destination, it's not necessary to be fully made up during your flight. If your skin feels dry, add a touch of moisturizer and then the appropriate foundation. Add your blush and brush on some compact powder.

Add your eyeshadow. You will find that a dark earthtone eyeshadow such as charcoal, brown, or plum applied subtly over the entire lid and smudged in the outer corners of your eye will give definition to your eyes. Then when you are at the terminal, add a touch of mascara and eye pencil.

Many women find that their skin becomes very dry while on a plane; and there is a reason for this. The pressurized cabin and conditioned air deplete the skin's natural moisture. Since your skin will probably show signs of dryness, make sure that you bring along a body lotion for your hands, in addition to your facial moisturizer.

An important note on applying your makeup: use a soft touch with all your makeup. The lights in the plane lavatories not only drain the color from your face, but often give a green-yellow cast to your skin. If you apply your makeup until you can see the color well under these conditions, you've most likely applied too much makeup for daylight.

If you are meeting someone immediately upon disembarking, your image will not suffer if your makeup is too soft, but you can give a bad impression if it is over-done or too harsh. After you have applied your makeup in the restroom, check it in the daylight if you have a window seat.

Traveling Tips
"Your Traveling Cosmetic Case"

If you travel frequently, you should have a bag set aside solely for business travel. Buy small plastic bottles into which you can easily put your standard skincare preparations. If you often have little advance notice before travel, you should keep the plastic bottles filled. In addition to your skincare and makeup products, include:

- tooth paste, dental floss and a toothbrush
- a comb and brush, curlers and setting lotion
- a shower cap, a razor, cotton swabs and balls
- deodorant and perfume

Is This Food Edible?

This may be a question you ask when faced with an airline meal. But you do have a choice. If it is a long flight you can bring your own. Or try calling at least a day in advance and the airline can create a special meal for you personally—if you are on a diet or have some food restrictions, be assertive. There is usually no charge, and the food is usually better than the standard fare.

Be cautious about drinking. An ounce of liquor in the air is equivalent to two ounces on the ground. And it typically takes about two hours for each ounce of liquor to go through your bloodstream. This means that if you have two drinks, you'll feel the effects for a minimum of four hours! Take this into consideration if you have business associates meeting you at the airport.

Exercises in the Air—Flyers Fitness Formula

Lufthansa Airlines is the first airline, and to our knowledge the only one, to create a series of exercises especially for plane rides! Concerned about the physical effects of sitting in the same seat for a long period of time, they developed an exercise program called *"Fitness in the Air"* to help passengers beat fatigue and arrive feeling fit and refreshed.

According to Lufthansa, this is very important for several reasons. Sitting inactive for long periods of time makes your body stiff, causes muscle tone deterioration, reduces coordination and flexibility of the joints, slows circulation, and reduces oxygen supply to your organs. No wonder we feel so terrible after a long flight!

Lufthansa recommends Muscle Tone Training as the ideal program for inflight exercise—it's inconspicuous, takes no extra time, and it keeps the musculature in shape. And most important—it can be done in your seat.

According to the Lufthansa medical experts, you should never sit in a chair too long. Stand up frequently and take a few steps to and fro. For this reason, consider selecting an aisle seat. While it may not afford you an interesting view, you will feel freer to leave your seat than if you have to keep climbing over several people. With the aisle seat you can also stretch your legs throughout the flight—another good exercise for the air.

Traveling Tips
"Fitness in the Air"

Tighten up a muscle or muscle group with about one-third of your maximum strength. Repeat six times. Exercise rhythmically.

Use systematically for those parts of the body particularly affected by long sitting:

Stomach:	To improve the tone of the stomach muscles, flex the abdomen with about one-third of your strength, holding this position for a few seconds, relaxing the muscles again and then repeating the exercise in rhythm several times. The relaxing part is just as important for training stimulus.

Then follow the same guideline for the following areas:

Thigh:	Left, then right.
Buttocks:	Left side, then right.
Back:	Left side, then right.
Shoulders:	Left, then right.

Fitness in the Air muscle tone training is invisible, so it can be performed anywhere, anytime.

Chapter 20

Executive Pregnancy—

With Style!

There is a New Woman in the executive office today, one who has come to grips with being a woman and a professional. One of the most obvious signs that she has arrived is the recent trend toward "professional motherhood." This is a relatively new role for the executive suite—in the old days the handful of executive women who did get pregnant traditionally opted for full-time motherhood and promptly retired. In fact, often before anyone was aware of their pregnancy, they were safely ensconced in the privacy of their home to await the "blessed event."

But that's not the case today. Many executive women are choosing both motherhood and career. In many cases they continue on with their work until a few weeks before the birth, and return to their job a few weeks after. The new mother's absence is often the equivalent of a month-long summer-type vacation as far as her work is concerned. I know a State Attorney General who left the office at her usual quitting time and had her baby later that night. Two weeks later she was back protecting consumers against fraud. And she was on the phone with her subordinates for most of those two weeks!

Timing

The timing of your pregnancy is of course, a personal decision. The trend recently has been for executive women to make their decision about children in their early thirties. This is only natural, since they are beginning to become aware of the "biological" time clock.

In other ways, this is probably the best time for the woman who wants both a career and a child. At this point in her life, the career woman should have solid business experience, which will make it easier for her to obtain a leave of absence from her current employer, or to re-enter the job market if she decides to quit.

The more valuable an employee you are, the more flexibility you can expect from your company. As a manager with clout, you will be able to schedule doctor's appointments, work-at-home days, and a mutually agreeable leave of absence. Check your company policy regarding maternity leave prior to discussing your leave with anyone in the company. The more definite you can make your plans before talking with your boss, the more he or she will think of your leave in temporary terms. If you are vague about how long you will be on leave and what your plans are, the company may think that you will not be returning.

Maintaining Your Image

The woman who tackles both roles must suddenly confront a number of image and style problems. One of the most important is how to maintain a sense of professional style. Many traditional maternity clothes are inexpensively made and designed to be utilitarian at best. (And let's face it, the underlying concepts of chic styling and maternity styling are often in direct contradiction). But the professional woman cannot afford to put her image on hold for four or five months while she wears inexpensive maternity clothes if she is really serious about her career. The first priority then is to develop a professional-looking maternity wardrobe, a problem made more complicated if she has a limited budget to work with.

Because men still are, and probably always will be, a bit uneasy around pregnant women, it is beneficial to the professional woman to develop a maternity wardrobe that emphasizes sleek lines and de-emphasizes her pregnancy. After all, you don't really want to send the meeting into a tailspin because unnerved men are unable to take their minds off the idea that the boss is pregnant.

I hope that none of the above is misunderstood. I am not suggesting that the expectant mother be less than proud of her condition. But let's face facts. Your impending motherhood is going to throw your male co-workers off-balance. This should be minimized, since I don't expect the American male executive to get his head on straight any time soon on matters of this sort. But you do have some control. And it is my personal opinion that the less they are reminded of your pregnancy, the fewer problems it is likely to cause.

Susan is a regional manager for a high-tech company just outside of Boston. She had her first child last year. She recalls one business meeting that she attended when she was seven months pregnant and "full with motherhood." "I was meeting with men from a department that I dealt with very infrequently. When I entered the room, I was greeted with wide eyes, open mouths, and silence. Then, all of a sudden there was a mad scramble to get me a chair and many hands trying to help me into it." She adds, "All of this, of course, I could have done without."

She passed on two suggestions from her experience. If you are attending an important meeting with a number of men who haven't seen you in your "new shape," drop by several of their offices to let them become accustomed to it. This is especially important if you have some important contributions to make at the meeting and don't want your "condition" to overshadow your presentation. And next, always dress in a manner that diminishes the impact of your pregnancy on your appearance. I hope that Susan's suggestions will gradually become unnecessary as more and more executive women continue to work during pregnancy.

Pregnancy with Panache

You can retain your professional style during your pregnancy without buying a completely new wardrobe. We've gathered some tips for maternity wear from those who have experienced it firsthand.

Many pregnant businesswomen prefer dresses during their pregnancy. The best are those without waistlines, that focus attention on the neckline via a bow, scarf, jewelry, or unusual collar. This dress will give the pregnant woman the comfort and freedom of movement she especially needs. There are no elasticized waistbands or tight bustlines to constrict her. For business meetings you can put a jacket on over it and still have a polished and professional look.

One additional benefit of this outfit is that you can wear the dress after the baby arrives. And you do not have to buy a new jacket—one of your unstructured jackets from non-maternity days will complete the look. Use a sash or a belt to add definition to its line and you have a non-maternity office dress.

Because many women experience problems with body temperature during pregnancy, I recommend dresses that are made of all natural fibers. Good colors for these are navy, black, or burgundy.

Another useful item is the jumper. It has the same benefits as the dress. You can wear a jumper with your pre-pregnancy blouses and have a comfortable new look. I recommend wearing a blazer with the jumper since this will give it a more professional appearance.

Separates

You can still achieve the more formal look of a suit by selecting separates that have roomy styles. This also enables you to wear them after the baby is born.

For example, look for long cardigan-type jackets that don't need to be buttoned. There are also a number of new style jackets that are loosely constructed so that they can be worn with or without a belt. They are not only perfect for work but ideal for you during and after pregnancy.

Many non-maternity skirts have an expandable waist or dropped waist. These skirts can see you through the initial pregnancy period and then after your pregnancy, too.

When you wear two-piece outfits, try coordinating them so that the lighter or brighter color is in the jacket and the darker more subdued color in the skirt. Visually, light colors draw attention—the eye is drawn up to the face and away from the mid-section. Look for blouses with bows or interesting necklines, again to focus attention on your face and away from your figure.

Accessories

Your accessories can play an important role in your maternity outfit. Not only will they diversify the number of looks available from the same basic outfits, they will also divert attention from your figure. Look especially for accessories that focus attention on your neckline and face area. Consider larger and longer earrings to give your face a slimming effect. Wear eye-catching necklaces. Look for bright scarves or floppy bows to enhance your neckline.

You should definitely avoid high-heeled shoes or strappy styles that provide little support. However, according to one obstetrician with whom I spoke, flats are not recommended. They will only increase the amount of pressure on your back—a slight heel will give you better balance, and better posture.

Extra
Edge

Skincare

During pregnancy, a woman's body undergoes many hormonal changes that can affect the skin, with varying results. Some women find that their skin has never been better. Others, however, are less fortunate and find themselves plagued with skin problems, many for the first time in their lives. Consider, for example, the plight of the thirty-five year old vice-president of public relations who had been virtually blemish-free during her teenage years and suddenly was confronted with a severe case of acne brought on by the bio-chemical changes of pregnancy.

While most women will not face such serious problems, pregnancy is a time for proper skincare and the right makeup program. Pay attention to your skin—you should realize from our discussion on skincare in a previous chapter that your skin will tell you what it needs.

Most women, during this time, will find that their skin becomes oilier due to an increase in estrogen levels. If your skin is getting oilier or shinier than usual, cut back on the amount of moisturizer you use. You may find that you should switch to a lighter moisturizer. If your skin begins to break out, I recommend switching to a water-base foundation until it normalizes.

Approach your skin problems accordingly if your skin suddenly becomes drier. Increase the amount of moisturizing. But don't overdo it. Remember, your skin should look and feel normal, not as if it has a slick of grease on it from too-heavy creams.

A word of caution if you are pregnant during the summer months. The changes in your body can make your skin susceptible to "mottling"—patches of increased pigmentation. Sunbathing or even walking outside can dramatically increase the pigmentation spots on your face. Make sure that you wear a strong sunscreen (SPF 10 or more) or even better, a sunblock (SPF 15) to prevent those spots of extra pigmentation from appearing.

Makeup

During your pregnancy, you should pay a little more attention to your makeup. At times during your pregnancy you may find yourself looking tired, drained, or pale. Makeup can help you to look as sparkly and glowing as nature intended. During this time it might be better to use a little more blush (in a very soft pink or mauve). Brush some across your nose, your cheeks, your forehead. This will simulate the type of color you would get from a few hours in the sunshine.

Hair

If ever you considered an easy-to-maintain hairstyle, now is the time to try it. You will find that both your skin and your hair react to the chemical changes in your body. Your hair may show signs of thinning or dullness or it may grow thicker and more luxuriant then ever.

If you have an easy-to-maintain hairstyle, it will make your life much less complicated during these months. Since you have put on weight, your face will probably appear much fuller than normal. Look for a hairstyle that will have a slimming effect on your face—perhaps one with waves or one that is swept back from your face.

Consider getting a permanent wave. It will save you a lot of time and you will know that your hair looks good. You are going to find that your work schedule and your motherhood plans will leave you little time for frequent trips to the hair salon. And you may not have quite your usual energy level, so simple things such as setting your hair on a daily basis may become an unwelcome chore.

One last word about Professional Style and your maternity. Remember, you don't have to sacrifice it while you are pregnant. With a little creativity you can have a maternity wardrobe that has as much élan as your regular working wardrobe. Most of all, your attitude and your appearance should be bright and positive—after all you are the New Executive Woman. And unlike most of the pioneering, first women executives, you will have it all—a career and a family!

Extra
Edge

203

Index

Look Successful, Be Successful

A Complete Guide to Professional Style

Order your own **Personalized Guide to Total Professional Style.**
Based on Charlene Mitchell's research, your guide will help you develop a new on-the-job image, tailored to your business, body, and professional needs. Your personalized guide will help you choose flattering clothing, makeup, hairstyles and colors, to enhance your appearance and promote your success.

For only $19.95 we'll send you a questionnaire designed to identify your assets and liabilities. Once you return the questionnaire, you will receive a personal analysis and comprehensive program—including clothing illustrations, makeup and skin care charts.

Invest in yourself and your career. Send for your guide TODAY!

☐ YES! I want to look successful. Please enroll me in Charlene Mitchell's Total Professional Style program.

Make check payable to: SAVOIR—"For Professional Women Only"

FREE!

Send for your complimentary issue of THE IMAGE TRENDSLETTER, a newsletter devoted to the latest trends in color, fashion, home interiors, imaging. Use this coupon to order a free copy NOW.

☐ YES! Please send me a complimentary issue of THE IMAGE TRENDSLETTER.

NAME_____

ADDRESS_____

_____ ZIP _____

Mail to:
SAVOIR
c/o ACROPOLIS BOOKS LTD.
2400 17th St., N.W.
Washington, D.C. 20009

Extra
Edge